KU-169-192

QUARKXPRESS

QUARK XPRESS

Christopher Lumgair

TEACH YOURSELF BOOKS

Trademarks

Many of the designations used by manufacturers and sellers to distinguish their products are claimed as trademarks. Where those designations appear in this book, and Hodder & Stoughton was aware of the trademark claim, the designations have been printed in initial caps or all caps.

Long-renowned as the authoritative source for self-guided learning – with more than 30 million copies sold worldwide – the *Teach Yourself* series includes over 200 titles in the fields of languages, crafts, hobbies, sports, and other leisure activities.

A catalogue record for this title is available from the British Library.

Library of Congress Catalog Card Number on file.

First published in UK 1997 by Hodder Headline Plc, 338 Euston Road, London NW1 3BH.

First published in US 1997 by NTC Publishing Group, 4255 West Touhy Avenue, Lincolnwood (Chicago), Illinois 60646 – 1975 U.S.A.

The 'Teach Yourself' name and logo are registered trade marks of Hodder & Stoughton Ltd in the UK

Copyright © 1997 Christopher Lumgair

In US: All rights reserved. No part of this publication may be reproduced or transmitted in any form or by any means, electronic or mechanical, including photocopy, recording, or any information storage and retrieval system, without permission in writing from the publisher or under licence from the Copyright Licensing Agency Limited. Further details of such licences (for reprographic reproduction) may be obtained from the Copyright Licensing Agency Limited, of 90 Tottenham Court Road, London W1P 9HE.

In US: All rights reserved. No part of this book may be reproduced, stored in a retrieval system, or transmitted in any form, or by any means, electronic, mechanical, photocopying, or otherwise, without prior permission of NTC Publishing Group.

Printed in England by Cox & Wyman Limited, Reading, Berkshire.

Impression number 10   9   8   7   6   5   4   3   2   1
Year   2000   1999 1998 1997

CONTENTS

7 Working with text boxes 69

Appendix III 177

Appendix IV 181

Index 191

1

INTRODUCTION

This book has a simple goal: to introduce complete beginners to desktop publishing and teach them the necessary skills with which to produce soundly-constructed and well-presented documents using QuarkXPress 3.3.

Publications on QuarkXPress tend to fall into two categories: either they are over sophisticated, comprehensible only to the initiated, or they are frustratingly simplistic. By combining simple step-by-step instructions with sound practical advice drawn from years of design and desktop publishing experience, I hope I have somehow struck a balance between these two extremes.

In integrating functions and technologies previously handled by different specialists, QuarkXPress, like other desktop publishing programs, has inevitably absorbed the terminology and processes of many disciplines including publishing, design, paste-up, reprographics and, naturally, computer technology.

As a result of this, great demands are placed on anyone working in DTP today. We need not only to use a DTP program skilfully but also to understand the processes, languages and disciplines involved in its use. With this in mind, I include appendices on points of style, typographic measurements, the document-making process and essential technical terms.

Whether you are new to the world of visual communications or a professional in the field, I hope you will find this a useful guide to a remarkable desktop publishing tool.

—— Overview of QuarkXPress ——

What is QuarkXPress?

QuarkXPress is a page layout program, providing the means by which all phases of document design and production can be accomplished. It offers text editing and typographical controls, it provides for the importation and accurate placement of images, it has automated features, such as master pages and style sheets and it has powerful printing and colour separation capabilities.

The pasteboard

QuarkXPress uses the concept of the 'pasteboard' – the artboard on which paste-up artists in the past created artwork for printing. Pages in QuarkXPress are delineated areas within pasteboards and when pages face each other, as spreads, they share the same pasteboard. There's a pasteboard for each page or set of facing pages and these pasteboards abut vertically to one another within the document window. As you scroll downwards through a document, you see each pasteboard in turn.

You can place items on pasteboards when you work but only items within page areas are printed.

Page grids

You set columns and margin sizes, amongst other things, at the start of a document. These settings define a master page, called Master A which provides the grid for the first document page and for any other pages you wish to create based on this master. Further master pages can be developed from the original setting to create pages with different grids.

You can place repeatedly-used items directly on master pages and these are automatically copied onto document pages. Some typical master page items are headers, footers and page numbers.

Items, text and images

Unlike in a word-processing document, you can't just type or enter images directly onto a QuarkXPress page. You enter text and images into special boxes which you place on pages as you work on a document. These boxes define the area, shape and position of text or images and are analogous to the precisely cut pieces of type matter and guides pasted onto traditional artboards.

Text attributes

You style text using character or paragraph attributes, much in the same way as you do in a word-processing program.

You can create style sheets, embodying full sets of text attributes to style paragraphs quickly and consistently.

Automatic hyphenation and the way paragraphs are justified are controlled by H&Js (hyphenation and justification).

Picture attributes

You can make modifications to imported images, to some extent, within QuarkXPress, but this work is best done in an image manipulation program, such as Adobe Photoshop.

You can also make up simple graphic elements using standard text or picture boxes, lines and polygons.

Printing

You can output documents on desktop printers for proofing and printing purposes. You can also image-set documents to bromide or film and produce colour separations ready for plate-making. QuarkXPress will automatically colour separate all imported images, whether they contain process or spot colours.

Conventions used in this book

Keystrokes in the main text are shown as icons, such as ⌘

When icons are separated by a + sign, as in ⌘ Alt Shift + Delete , the modifier key(s) before the + sign should be held down together, whilst the key after the + sign is pressed.

Some keyboards include an Option instead of the Alt key.

QuarkXPress items, such as text or picture boxes, are illustrated as they appear on screen, often with guides and invisibles showing.

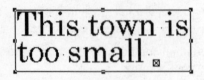

Other margin icons in this book are used in the following contexts.

● Single-step instructions and key points.

① Step-by-step instructions.

! Warnings and critical information.

▲ Helpful hints.

✚ Additional non-essential information.

2

THE QUARKXPRESS INTERFACE

This chapter covers:

- the scroll bars, menu and dialog boxes
- the Tool palette
- the Measurements palette

QuarkXPress interface

This chapter is intended as a general reference to three key features of QuarkXPress, namely the QuarkXPress document window and the Tool and Measurements palettes.

For those new to the Macintosh, the final sub-section covers the standard Macintosh controls used within the program.

You may wish to just peruse this chapter and move on, refering back to it as and when necessary.

— Document window and palettes —

The document window

The document window displays an open QuarkXPress document.
Features include:

①   title bar

②   close box

③   zoom box

④   size box

⑤   document page, with pasteboard area

⑥   scroll bars

⑦   rulers

⑧   ruler origin

⑨   view percent field

⑩   page number indicator

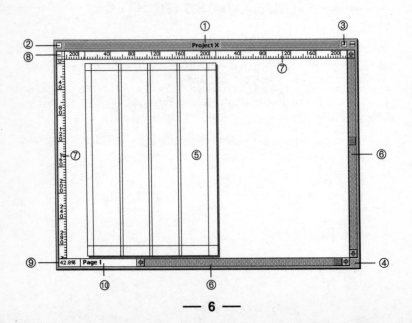

The tool palette

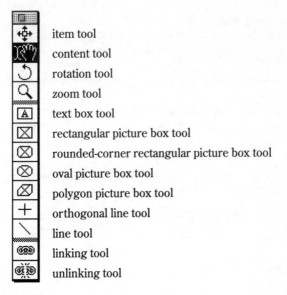

item tool

content tool

rotation tool

zoom tool

text box tool

rectangular picture box tool

rounded-corner rectangular picture box tool

oval picture box tool

polygon picture box tool

orthogonal line tool

line tool

linking tool

unlinking tool

Using the tool palette

Selecting a tool

●   Click once on a tool icon and then release the mouse button.

The tool you select determines what you can do with the mouse and the keyboard and which menu and menu commands are available.

The measurements palette

Options in the measurements palette

Text box selected (left end)

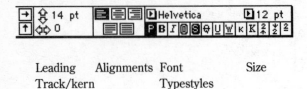

Hor. position	Box width	Box angle	Flip hor.
Vert. position	Box height	No. of columns	Flip vert.

Text box selected with the Content tool active (right end)

Leading	Alignments	Font		Size
Track/kern		Typestyles		

Picture box selected (left end)

Hor. position	Box width	Box angle	Flip hor.
Vert. position	Box height	Corner radius	Flip ver.

Picture box selected with the Content tool active (right end)

→ X%:100%	⇔ X+:0 mm	△ 0°
↑ Y%:100%	⬍ Y+:0 mm	▱ 0°

Image width   Hor. image position   Image angle
Image height Vert. image position Image skew

Using the measurements palette

The measurements palette is an alternative control that can be used
for applying many text, picture and line attributes. Specifications are
entered into the palette in a number of ways.

Entering new values in fields

① Double-click existing values (if not already highlighted).

② Type in new values.

▲ To enter pt in mm fields, type in p and then the figure (such as p72) or the
figure then pt (such as 72pt).

To enter mm in pt fields, type in the figure followed by m (such as 6m).

Moving from field to field

● Press [Tab]

Selecting options from pop-up menus

Either:

● point to the small triangle by the pop-up menu, press to 'pop
up' the menu, drag to the item you wish to choose so that it's
highlighted and then release the mouse button.

Or:

● position the insertion point in the field, type in the first letters
of the item to be chosen.

Applying specifications in fields

● Press [Return] or [Enter ↵]

—————— **Macintosh basics** ——————

Scroll bars

Every window has two scroll bars, one for vertical scrolling and one for horizontal scrolling. A grey scroll bar indicates that there is more content beyond a window's borders; a clear bar indicates that all contents are visible.

Using the scroll bars

Either:

● click the up, down, left or right scroll arrow.

Or:

● click the vertical or horizontal scroll bar on either side of the scroll box, when it's grey.

Or:

● drag the vertical or horizontal scroll box along its scroll bar.

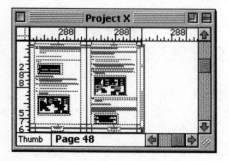

▲   You can set the scrolling performance in the Application Preferences dialog box. You can adjust the scrolling speed and enable/disable Speed Scroll and Live Scroll. Speed Scroll greeks images and blends temporarily so you can move from page to page more quickly. Live Scroll updates the document view as you drag a scroll bar. You can also enable/disable Live Scroll temporarily by pressing Alt when you scroll.

Menus

Macintosh menus come in two types: pull-down menus and pop-up menus. The menus in the QuarkXPress menu bar are pull-down menus. Pop-up menus often appear in palettes and dialog boxes.

Selecting options from pull-down menus

●   Point to the menu name, press to 'pull down' the menu, drag to the item you wish to choose so that it's highlighted and then release the mouse button.

Dialog boxes

Specifications are entered into dialog boxes in a number of ways.

Entering new values

①   Double-click existing values (if not already highlighted).

②   Type in new values.

▲   To enter pt in mm fields, type in p and then the figure (such as p72) or the figure then pt (such as 72pt).

   To enter mm in pt fields, type in the figure followed by m (such as 6m).

Moving from field to field

●   Press Tab

Selecting options from pop-up menus

●   Point to the visible menu item, press to 'pop up' the additional menu, drag to the item you wish to choose so that it's highlighted and then release the mouse button.

Checking boxes

● Click box. An X indicates its selected.

Clicking radio buttons

● Click button. A emboldened button indicates it's selected.

Applying specifications

● Click Apply. The dialog box will remain displayed.

Applying specifications and closing box

● Click OK or press [Return] or [Enter ↵]

▲ Hold down the Alt key and click Apply to see the effect of changes when the tab key is pressed or a new field clicked. Hold down the Alt key and click Apply to disable the function.

3

CREATING AND
SAVING DOCUMENTS

This chapter covers

- the New Document and Open dialog boxes
- the Save As directory dialog box
- the Application Preferences dialog box

Creating documents

Starting a new document

Loading QuarkXPress

- Double-click on the QuarkXPress™ program icon within the QuarkXPress folder on your hard disk.

The QuarkXPress menu will be displayed.

⬛ File Edit Style Item Page View Utilities

❗ There is no need to double-click the icon if it's greyed as this indicates that QuarkXPress is already loaded on the RAM.

Starting a new document

① Choose Document in the New sub-menu in the File menu. The New Document dialog box will be displayed.

❗ If the QuarkXPress menu is not showing, choose QuarkXPress in the Applications menu at the far right of the menu bar.

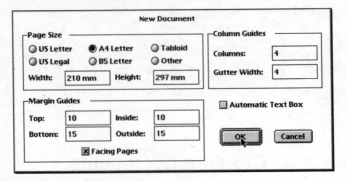

② Click a standard page size or enter values in the Width and Height fields.

③ Either: check the Facing Pages box if your document has a central spine (or fold) and you are printing on both the left and right-hand pages.

Or: uncheck the Facing Pages box if you are printing only on, say, the right-hand pages of a document or if your document has multiple folds.

④ Enter values in the margin fields, number of columns fields and gutter field.

⑤ Uncheck Automatic Text Box (in all cases).

⑥ Click OK. The document window will be displayed.

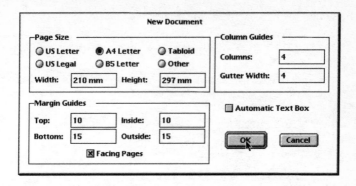

▲   When you are entering values into fields in dialog boxes, it's best to double-click the existing values to highlight them, and then to enter the new value to overwrite them, either including the units of measure or not. All the entries in the following example are acceptable.

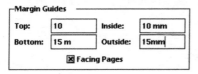

Saving documents

Saving a new document

Before you do any work in your new document, give it a name and save it to disk.

①   Chose Save… in the File menu. The Save As directory dialog box will be displayed.

②   Enter a document name, overwriting the name Untitled 1.

③   Select a drive and folder in which to save the file.

④   Click the Document radio button.

⑤   Click Save to save a document. Click Cancel if you wish to abort the routine.

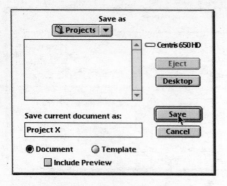

▲ Resave every five minutes or so whilst you are working on a document, always using the Save command. The Save As directory dialog box will not be displayed on subsequent saves.

Although you can use up to 31 characters in a file name, it's best to restrict yourself to around twenty so that names show in full within directory dialog boxes.

Enabling Auto Saves

You can specify that QuarkXPress automatically creates a temporary Auto Save file whilst you are working on a document. Should your system crash for any reason, this Auto Save file will survive intact and substitute for your original file which may be damaged. For peace of mind, it's advisable to have Auto Save enabled at all times.

Don't go looking for the Auto Save when your document is closed, as the Auto Save file won't exist. If you wish to check if Auto Save is working, look for it in the folder in which your working file is saved using the Open directory dialog box.

When you open an Auto Save file after a system crash, you are given the opportunity to revert back to any manual save you made since the Auto Save was last updated.

Specifying Auto Save

① Choose Application... in the Preferences sub-menu in the Edit menu. The Application Preferences dialog box will be displayed.

② Check the Auto Save box and enter a value, such as 5, in the Every...Minutes box.

③ Click OK.

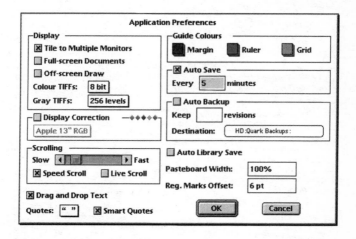

Keeping revisions

You can specify that QuarkXPress automatically creates 'historical' backups of a document each time you manually save.

Each time you save, the oldest backup is automatically deleted as a new backup is made to maintain a specified number of backups.

Specifying Auto Backup

① Choose Application... in the Preferences sub-menu in the Edit menu. The Application Preferences dialog box will be displayed.

② Check the Auto Backup box and enter a value, such as 2, in Keep...revisions box.

③ Click the Destination button. The Backup Destination dialog box will be displayed.

④ Locate a folder in which to create a special backup folder. Click the New folder button.

⑤ Enter Quark Backups or similar in the Name field. Click OK.

⑥ Click Select. You will be returned to the Application Preferences dialog box. Note the new destination path on the Destination button.

⑦ Click OK.

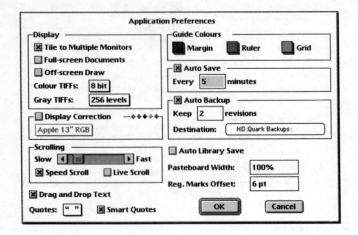

!   Auto Backups are not adequate substitutes for copies of documents you make yourself at various intervals, under different names, using the File/Save as… routine.

— Opening and closing documents —

Opening an existing document

Either:

① choose Open... in the QuarkXPress's File menu. The Open directory dialog box will be displayed.

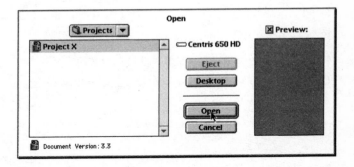

** File Edit Style Item Page View Utilities**

If the QuarkXPress menu is not showing, choose QuarkXPress in the Applications menu at the far right of the menu bar. If it is not listed, load QuarkXPress. See *Loading QuarkXPress* (page 13).

② Use the directory dialog box controls to locate your document.

③ Click Open. The document window will be displayed.

Or:

● double-click on its document icon in its Finder window on the desktop. The document window will be displayed.

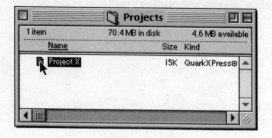

✛   If QuarkXPress has not already been loaded on the RAM it will now be loaded. Its title and menu bar will soon be displayed.

Creating a copy of an open document

Use this process to create and move to a copy of a document or to create a template.

①   Chose Save As… in the File menu. The Save As directory dialog box will be displayed.

②   Enter a document name, overwriting its existing name.

③   Select a drive and folder in which to save the file.

④   Click the Document (or Template) radio button.

⑤   Click Save to save a document. Click Cancel if you wish to abort the routine.

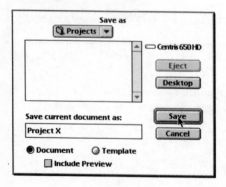

! If you wish the closing document to contain all your latest work, choose Save... in the File menu first and then choose Save As...

! Click Template only if you wish to save a file for repeated use. (See page 183). Templates are partially completed documents, including master pages, document pages, items, text and images, H&Js, style sheets and colours common to all issues of the document.

Closing a document

① Click the Close box at the top left of the document window.

② An alert box saying 'Save the new document "..."?' or 'Save changes to document "..."?' will be displayed.

③ Click OK to save the document. Click No if you do not wish to save a new document or recent work.

Quitting QuarkXPress

① Choose Quit in the File menu.

② An alert box saying 'Save the new document "..."?' or 'Save changes to document "..."?' will be displayed if your document is still open and recent work has not been saved.

③ Click OK to save the document. Click No if you do not wish to save a new document or recent work.

Summary

● All new documents are started by choosing New Document in QuarkXPress's File menu.

● Open a saved document within the Finder window or by choosing Open in QuarkXPress's File menu.

● Always give a new document a descriptive name, preferably no longer than 20 characters.

● Neither Auto Save nor Auto Backup are substitutes for manually saved versions under different names.

4

WORKING WITH DOCUMENT PAGES

This chapter covers

- the Document Layout palette
- the Page menu
- the View menu
- the Document Setup dialog box
- the General Preferences dialog box
- rulers and ruler guides

—— Working with document pages ——

A new QuarkXPress document is based on settings entered by you in the New dialog box. These settings are used to specify page size, margin and column guides.

The margin and column guide settings define a master page (called Master A). This master page provides the grid for the first and any additional document pages.

The page size setting in the New dialog box defines the document as a whole.

Creating and deleting document pages

Creating document pages individually

① Choose Document Layout in the View menu. The Document Layout palette will be displayed.

② Click once on the icon to the left of A-Master A in the palette. The master page icon will turn black.

③ Click-drag the icon downwards into the document page window of the palette.

④ Release the mouse button when the pointer turns into a page icon.

Non-Facing Pages   Facing Pages

Creating a range of document pages

① Choose Insert... in the Page menu. The Insert Pages dialog box will be displayed.

② Enter a value in the Insert Pages field, click on the After Page radio button and enter 1 in the field to its right.

③ Choose A-Master A in the Master Page pop-up menu.

④ Click OK.

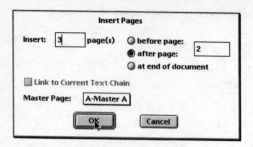

Deleting document pages individually

① Choose Document Layout in the View menu. The Document Layout palette will be displayed.

② Click once on the document page icon in the palette. The page icon will turn black.

③ Click once on the Delete Page icon at the top right of the palette. An alert box will be displayed saying 'Are you sure you wish to remove these pages?'.

④ Click OK.

Deleting a range of document pages

① Choose Delete… in the Page menu. The Delete Pages dialog box will be displayed.

②   Enter the range of pages you wish to delete in the Delete page(s) and thru fields.

③   Click OK.

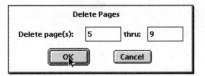

!   Enter in editorial, not 'absolute' numbers, when deleting pages. Editorial numbers are the numbers which appear at the bottom left of the document window. These may differ from the numbers in the Document Layout palette if you have altered the numbering in any way. See *Managing page numbers* (page 87).

——— Making changes ———

Moving document pages

Moving document pages individually

①   Either: choose Document Layout in the View menu. The Document Layout palette will be displayed.

     Or: choose Thumbnails… in the View menu.

②   Use the scroll bars in each case until the page concerned is in view.

③   Click-drag the page to be moved to its new position. Release the mouse button when the small arrow appears within the adjacent document page.

④   The page will move and the other pages will shuffle along.

⑤   If working with Thumbnails, choose another scale in the View menu to continue your work.

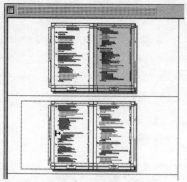
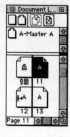

Thumbnails view   Document Layout
                                         palette

▲   You can click-drag pages from one document to another if both documents
    are open, in Thumbnail view and tiled within the screen. When you do this a
    copy of a page is moved, not the original.

Moving a range of document pages

①   Choose Move… in the Page menu. The Move Pages dialog
    box will be displayed.

②   Enter values in the Move page(s) and thru fields and click a
    radio button. Enter a page number in the field to the right.

③   Click OK.

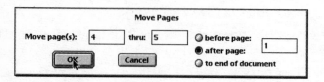

▲   When inserting, deleting and moving pages, unless a document's left and
    right margins are of equal width, try to avoid moving pages from one side of
    the spine to the other side, in other words from left to right and vice versa. If
    a documents margin guides are unequal in width, items correctly positioned
    on a left-hand page will be out of position on a right-hand page.

Changing a document's page size

①   Choose Document Setup… in the File menu. The Document Setup dialog box will be displayed.

②   Enter a new page size by clicking a radio button or by entering values in the Width and Height fields.

③   Click OK.

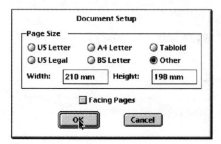

❗   If you are reducing the page size significantly, move all items towards the top left of each page before changing the size. Otherwise QuarkXPress may not allow the page size alteration to take place.

Changing the column and margin guide settings

①   Choose Document Layout in the View menu.

②   Double-click the icon to the left of A-Master A. Master A will then be displayed. A broken Link icon at the top left of a page indicates the page is a master page.

③   Choose Master Guides… in the Page menu.

④   Enter new values in the Master guides and Column guides fields.

⑤   Click OK.

⑥   Choose Document in the Display sub-menu in the Page menu.

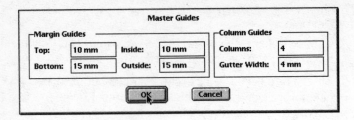

Working with pages

Viewing at different scales

Scaling a page to fit the document window

●   Choose Fit in Window in the View menu.

▲   Hold down the Alt key if you wish the pasteboard to fit to the window.

Changing the viewing scale of a page by pre-defined increments

①   Select the Zoom tool (or hold down [Control]) and click anywhere within the page to increase the viewing scale. Hold down [Alt] at the same time to reduce the viewing scale.

②   Reselect the Item tool or Content tool to deselect the Zoom tool (if selected from the tool palette).

Enlarging a specific area of a page

①   Select the Zoom tool (or hold down [Control]) and click-drag diagonally to define the area on the page to be enlarged.

②   Reselect the Item tool or Content tool to deselect the Zoom tool (if selected from the tool palette).

Viewing pages from two documents at a time

①   Open both documents in the usual way.

② Choose Tile Documents in the Windows sub-menu in the View menu.

Moving around a document

You can move around a document using the Document Layout palette, the scroll bars or the grabber hand.

Moving quickly from page to page

Either:

● double-click the relevant page icon within the Document Layout palette.

Or:

● click on either scroll bar either side of the scroll box with the view set to Fit in Window.

Moving a page within the document window

Either:

● hold down [Alt] and click-drag the page with the grabber hand icon.

Or:

● use the scroll bars.

Hiding/displaying non-printing items

Guides, rulers, invisibles and the Tool, Measurements and Document Layout palettes should be visible when you work.

Showing guides, rulers, Invisibles, and all palettes

● Choose Show Guides (or other command) in the View menu. If the item is already showing the word Hide will replace Show in the command so there is no need to choose the command.

Hiding guides, rulers, Invisibles, and all palettes

●   Choose Hide Guides (or other command) in the View menu.
If the item is already hidden the word Show will replace Hide
in the command so there is no need to choose the command.

Altering the ruler units

Each ruler can be calibrated in any one of seven measurements
units. For most work, it is usual to work in millimetres and/or
points.

Altering the measures

①   Select General... in the Preferences sub-menu in the Edit
menu or press ⌘ + Y . The General Preferences dialog
box will be displayed.

②   Select Millimetres or Points in the Horizontal and Vertical
Measures pop-up menus.

③   Click OK.

Adding ruler guides

Non-printing ruler guides can be added to any page or spread to
delineate the major alignments and principal areas in your layouts.
These guides are shown in green to differentiate them from the red
margin and column guides.

①   Choose Show Guides, Rulers and Measurements, in turn, in
the View menu. If any items are already showing the word
Hide will replace Show in the command so there is no need to
choose the command.

②   Click-drag from somewhere in the middle of either ruler to a
position within the document (or master) page. As you are
dragging, view the X or Y field in the Measurements palette.
Release the mouse button when you have reached the correct
position.

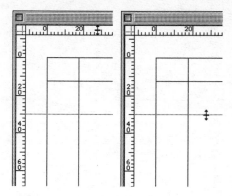

▲   Choose a viewing scale above 200% to position guides with greater accuracy.

Click-drag to a position on the pasteboard to create ruler guides which run across adjacent pages.

The X-coordinate normally measures from the left edge of pages, the Y-coordinate measures from the top edge of pages.

Margin, column and ruler guides can run either behind or in front of items on a page. Choose In Front or Behind in the Guides pop-up menu in the General Preferences dialog box.

Moving the ruler zero points

You can measure items from a point other than from the top and left edges of a document page. You do this by moving the ruler zero points.

You can print large document pages in sections by moving the ruler zero points. See *Printing large document pages* (page 160).

①   Click-drag from the small square at the junction of the rulers to a position within the document page.

②   Release the mouse button. The zero points will have moved accordingly.

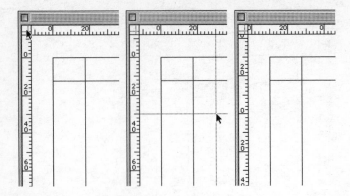

▲ Click once within the same square to return the zero points to their original position.

Summary

● Document pages are managed within Page menu dialog boxes and the Document Layout palette.

● Care needs to be taken when adding or deleting single pages in Facing Pages documents.

● Guides should be visible when creating page layouts.

● Ruler guides enable you to mark out major alignments.

● New pages should be based on Master A in simple grid documents.

5

ADDING TEXT

—— Working with text boxes ——

Text boxes within QuarkXPress are equivalent to the areas where typeset text is pasted down in conventional artwork. You place text in these boxes which you create on document pages as you work.

Text boxes define the dimensions of each area of text, and their size and position, together with picture boxes, determine the page layout.

Text boxes are often aligned with margin, column or ruler guides for accurate positioning.

You can place as many text boxes as you like on a document page. They can be altered in size at any time and the text within them can be changed.

▲   Although text boxes can be overlapped, keep text boxes well apart initially to prevent text from being displaced or disappearing.

Creating and resizing text boxes

Creating a text box

①   Select the Text box tool by clicking once only on its icon in the Tool palette.

②   Move the mouse (without pressing the button) over to the page. The pointer turns into a cross hair. Move the cross hair to where you wish the top left of the box to be (marked A).

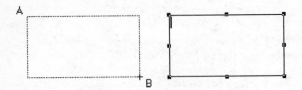

③   Click-drag (press the mouse button and move the mouse with the button depressed) diagonally to where you wish the bottom right corner of the box to be (marked B). Release the mouse button.

A flashing insertion point will be present at the top left of the box. When a text box is too small to accommodate any/all text, a small checked box appears within the text box.

④   If a checked box is displayed deepen the text box, by resizing it. If the insertion point is still not present, select, by clicking once with the mouse, the Content tool.

Resizing a text box

① With either the Item tool or Content tool active, click once somewhere within the box (if it is not already selected) and move the pointer to one of the handles at the bottom of the text box. Don't press the mouse button when you do this.

② The pointer turns into a pointing hand. While the pointing hand is displayed, click-drag the handle to resize the box.

▲ Handles halfway along the side of boxes can be used to enlarge or reduce a box in one direction only. Corner handles enable you to enlarge or reduce a box in two directions at once.

Enlarging or reducing a box, with the Command key held down, dynamically alters the scale of text within a box.

After a text box is created, the Item or Content tool will automatically be reselected, depending on which one was in use last.

Snap to Guides provides a fast and accurate way to align items to margin, column and ruler guides. Choose Snap to Guides in the View menu (to tick command, if not already ticked).

Moving and deleting text boxes

Moving a text box or other item

● With the Item tool active, click-drag the middle of the item.

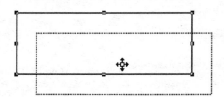

Deleting a text box or other item

Either:

● with the Item tool active, press [Delete].

Or:

● with either the Content tool or Item tool active, choose Delete in the Item menu.

▲ To move an item whilst the Content tool is active, hold down the Command key whilst click-dragging the item.

Entering text

You can enter text into text boxes by using the keyboard; by importing from a WP file or by using the Apple Clipboard. We cover the first two methods here. See Basic text editing for the use of the Apple Clipboard (page 40).

Keying in text

Entering text

① With the Content tool active, select a text box (if one is not already selected).

② Type in text using the keyboard.
If you are unable to see the text and a small checked box is displayed within the box, deepen the box.

If you are unable to see the text because the text appears as a grey line (called greeking), use the Zoom tool to view the text at a readable size.

NEW FONT RELEASE

from MultiVariant Inc

Lungari

Recently made available in PostScript, Campagna is a highly distinctive typeface designed for MultiVariant Inc by world-renowned font designer Angelo Lungari. It was designed from the start in three weights (book, medium and bold) with italic variants. Campagna is the ideal choice for advertising and magazine typography.

PostScript volumes 2304 and 2305 for Macintosh and PC

Special offer

The complete Campagna family at an introductory discount

Entering text, returns and spaces

You will find it easier to enter text accurately with the Invisibles showing; the symbols which represent non-printing characters, such as spaces or returns.

Text will automatically wrap when it reaches the right edge of a text box so there is no need to use a return at the end of each line.

Type in upper and lower case at all times. Capitals can be applied later using the Style menu or Measurements palette. Without a special Xtension, capitals cannot be turned into upper and lower case without rekeying text.

Showing invisbles

● Choose Show Invisibles in the View menu.

Starting a new paragraph

● Press Return

Starting a new line within a paragraph

Use these keystrokes to control line breaks within such text as a heading, address or verse.

● Press Shift + Return

Entering a normal word space

● Press Space

Show·Invisibles·when·you·type.·Text·
will·automatically·wrap·when·it·
reaches·the·right·edge·of·a·text·box.·.
Separate·paragraphs·using·this¶
Separate·lines·within·paragraphs·
using·this↵
Tab·using·this→   ¶
Type·in·Upper·and·Lowerlower·case·
and·not·in·CAPITALS.

▲ Check Smart Quotes in the Application Preferences dialog box so that the quotation marks you type are typographically correct.

Importing text from a WP file

Text can be imported from most word-processing (and ASCII) files. QuarkXPress imports all the text in a file, complete with page breaks etc. You may wish to bring in only part of a document. If so, copy and paste the text using the Apple Clipboard or split the word-processing document into a number of smaller documents first and then import text from each file in turn.

Importing text

①   With the Content tool active, select a text box (if one is not already selected).

②   Choose Get Text… in the File menu. The Get Text directory dialog box will be displayed.

③   Check the Convert Quotes box.

④   Use the directory dialog box controls to locate the text file.

⑤   Click OK.

!   Importing depends on the presence of the appropriate WP import filter in the XTension folder in the QuarkXPress folder.

▲   When importing text to be distributed amongst many text boxes, import the text into a temporary text box positioned to one side of the page. Then cut and paste the text from this box into the relevant text boxes. Delete the temporary text box after use.

Seeing all text in a text box

If text is overfilling a text box, a small checked box will be displayed. The presence of this box indicates that not all text is visible. It's good practice to make adjustments to remove the box even if the only hidden text comprises paragraph returns.

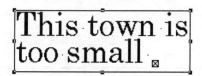

Showing all text in a box

① With the Content tool active, select a text box (if one is not already selected).

② Either: deepen or widen the text box.

Or: shorten the text. See *Basic Text Editing* (below).

Or: alter the text attributes. See *Formatting text* (page 46).

Basic text editing

You edit text within QuarkXPress in much the same way as you do in most word processors. You select the text and then add or delete text using the keyboard and copy or move text using the Clipboard.

Selecting text

Text needs to be selected for editing and formatting purposes. Text is selected using the Content tool which is the primary editing tool. When this tool is active, the pointer automatically turns into an I Beam when positioned over a text box.

In all cases, click once on text box to select box first, if not already selected.

Text to be selected	Number of clicks
● Any contiguous text	Click-drag over text.
● Whole word (with space after)	Click twice on word.
● Whole line	Click three times in line.
● Whole paragraph	Click four times within paragraph.
● All text in box (incl. hidden text)	Click five times in box or choose Select All in the Edit menu.

Selected characters in text are highlighted in colour.

> These characters have
> been selected whilst
> these characters havn't.

▲ When clicking to select text, try to click to a regular beat and keep the body of the mouse steady. If you are unable to click fast enough for selections to take place, select a slower Double-Click speed in the Mouse Control Panel in the Apple menu.

If you avoid clicking within a text box after you have finished your editing and formatting work and return to the text box later on, the text will retain its selection. If you wish it to forget its selection, click once within the box.

Click-dragging from the right of and level with the last line of a paragraph will select text without selecting the Return mark at the end of a paragraph (¶).

Moving and copying text using the Clipboard

Moving and copying text is normally done using the Apple Clipboard (a short-term storage area assigned for this purpose). Any text which you cut or copy is automatically placed on the Clipboard.

However many times you paste, text will remain on the Clipboard until another piece of text is cut or copied.

▲ The current contents of the Clipboard can be viewed at any time by choosing View Clipboard in the Edit menu.

Moving text

① Select the text you wish to move, by using one of the methods described previously. Choose Cut in the Edit menu.

② Position the insertion point where you wish to place the text (make sure it's 'blinking' within the text box) and select Paste in the Edit menu.

Copying text

① Select the text you wish to copy. Choose Copy in the Edit menu.

② Position the insertion point where you wish to place the copied text and select Paste in the Edit menu.

Deleting text

Either:

● select the text and press [Delete]

Or:

● position the insertion point to one side of the text to be deleted and press either [Delete] or [⌦]

Adding in extra text

① Position the insertion point where you wish to add text.

② Type in the additional text.

▲ If you select text instead of positioning the insertion point and choose Paste in the Edit menu, the pasted text will replace the selected text.

Text within a text box can be moved using a Drag and Drop technique similar to that available in Microsoft Word. Check the Drag and Drop box in the Application Preferences dialog box if you wish to use this technique.

Finding and replacing text

If you wish to change all instances of a word, or set of words, to something else (e.g. change 'the EEC' to 'Europe') use the Find/Change function within the Edit menu.

This function can save you longwinded editing work but approach this global function with great care. It's easy, through lack of planning, to alter text incorrectly – creating more work putting things right than it would otherwise have taken to alter the text manually in the first place.

Finding and replacing text

① Either: position the insertion point at the start of a text box to find and replace text in a story (all the text in a text box).

Or: do not select a text box at all to find and replace all text in a document.

② Choose Find/Change... in the Edit menu.

③ Type in the text to be found in the Find what field and replacement text in the Change to field.
Check the Document box if you wish to change text within the whole document. Check Whole Word if you wish the search to be limited to whole words.

④ Click Find Next to find the first instance of the text and click Replace you if wish to replace the word(s).

⑤ Click Find Next again and repeat the process until all instances of the text have been replaced.

⑥ Close the dialog box when finished.

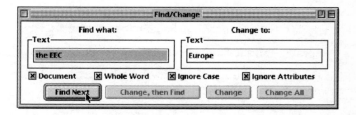

▲ When changing words globally using the Find/Change dialog box, always save the document first. Should you make an error when globally changing text, choose Revert to Saved in the File menu to return the document to its status before the changes were made.

Checking spelling

① Either: position the insertion point within a word to check the spelling of a single word.

Or: position the insertion point at the start of a text box to check the spelling of a story (all the text in a text box).

Or: do not select any text box at all to check the spelling of an entire document.

② Choose Check Spelling... in the Utilities menu.

③ Click OK when the Word Count panel box is displayed to display the Check (Word/Story/Document) dialog box.

④ A Suspect word will be identified, if any.

Either: click Suggest for a suggested correct spelling. Click on your preferred suggested spelling, if any.

Or: type in the correct spelling yourself in the Replace With field.

⑤ Click Replace.

⑥ The next Suspect word will be identified, if any.

⑦ Repeat step 5 and 6 until all the suspect words are corrected.

⑧ Click Cancel when finished or wait until it's checked all the words.

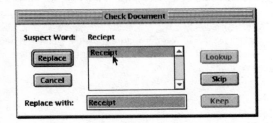

▲ Choose a view of 150% or above and ensure no palettes obscure the main part of the document window before checking spelling so you are able to see 'suspect' words in context.

Summary:

- Text boxes contain text and define text areas.

- Text can be imported into text boxes or typed in directly.

- Text selection methods allow you to select any amount of contiguous text within a text box.

- Moving and copying text is mainly done by means of the Apple Clipboard.

- Spelling can be checked on a word, story or document basis and text changes made globally.

6

FORMATTING TEXT

This chapter covers:

● the Style menu

● the Paragraph Formats dialog box

● the Rules dialog box

● the Paragraph Tabs dialog box

● the Style palette

Basic formatting

To meet your design needs, all the text you enter into text boxes will need to be given basic formatting, including such attributes as font, size, leading and alignment.

These attributes are applied using the Style menu, whilst text is selected. Some attributes can also be applied using the Measurements palette. See *Using the Measurements palette* (page 9).

Applying essential attributes

① Select the text to be styled using one of the methods described under *Selecting text* (page 40).

②   Choose a font in the Font sub-menu in the Style menu.

③   Choose a size in the Size sub-menu in the Style menu.

④   Choose an option (if required) in the Type Style sub-menu in the Style menu.

⑤   Choose Leading… in the Style menu. Enter a leading value in the Leading dialog box equal to or slightly greater than the type size. For normal text sizes (9 – 11 pt), the leading is usually 1 – 2 pt greater than the font size.

⑥   Choose Left, Centred, Right or Justified in the Alignment sub-menu in the Style menu.

▲   If fonts on the screen appear jagged at large sizes, you are probably using Adobe Type 1 fonts. These fonts need Adobe Type Manager to draw the fonts sharply on the screen. Adobe Type Manager (ATM) is available from Adobe and most computer mail order houses.

▲   It makes sense to apply any common or dominant style attributes in one operation. Select *all* the text in a box and apply these attributes. Other attributes can then be applied to just parts of the text. You are less likely to leave any text unstyled working this way and it's far quicker.

✦   Auto leading, the default leading value, is useful when initially sizing type, as it self adjusts to suit the font size. However, once you have chosen the font size, specify a value in points, unless there is only a single line of text in a box. In this case, leading is not implemented and you might as well leave it in Auto.

—————— Formatting paragraphs ——————

Formatting can be applied to characters or paragraphs within QuarkXPress. Character attributes can apply to all text within a box or to just one character, whilst paragraph attributes always apply to whole paragraphs or multiples of paragraphs.

Leading and alignment settings are paragraph attributes, as are indents, drop caps, spaces, rules and tabs.

Some settings for paragraphs can be entered in any one of seven units of measurement but are best entered in points as amounts are often based on font sizes and leading values.

Unless the horizontal and vertical measures are changed to points within the General Preferences dialog box, most attribute fields within dialog boxes and the measurements palette will be in millimetres (mm) apart, of course, from those relating to font size and leading. You can enter amounts in points in these fields; QuarkXPress will automatically convert the amounts to mm. The resulting conversion can be a bit confusing when you later review the settings.

▲   To enter pt in mm fields, type in p and then the figure (such as p72) or the figure then pt (such as 72pt).

To enter mm in pt fields, type in the figure followed by m (such as 6m).

Selecting paragraphs

Paragraphs are selected using one of the methods described below, with the Content tool active. If you wish to apply character attributes along with paragraph attributes, select the text using one of the methods described under *Selecting text* (page 37).

In all cases, click once on the text box, if it is not already selected.

Paragraphs to be selected	Method
● Whole paragraph	Either: place insertion point in text. Or: click four times within paragraph.
● Adjoining paragraphs	Click-drag over paragraphs; it's not necessary to select the whole area of a paragraph.
● All paragraphs in a text box (including hidden text)	Click five times in the text box or choose Select All in the Edit menu.

Selected paragraphs are partly highlighted in colour.

Although they are not fully
highlighted, both these paragraphs
have been selected.¶
Although they are not fully
highlighted, both these paragraphs
have been selected.

▲   Paragraphs in QuarkXPress are separated by Returns. To see these
    Returns for accurate selection, choose Show Invisibles in the View menu.
    The symbol for a Return is '¶'.

Indenting first lines of paragraphs

First line indents are conventionally used to identify paragraph
starts except for first paragraphs which are usually set full out.

Make tooth-like notches
in; form deep recesses in
(coastline etc.). Divide (doc

①   Select a paragraph or paragraphs using one of the methods
    previously described.

②   Choose Formats... in the Style menu. The Paragraph
    Formats dialog box will be displayed.

③   Enter a value in the First Line field.

④   Click Apply to see the effect. Click OK to implement the
    settings.

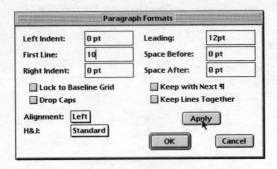

▲   Hold down the Alt key and click Apply to see the effect of changes when the
tab key is pressed or a new field clicked. Hold down the Alt key and click
Apply to disable the function.

Indenting both sides of paragraphs

Left and right indents may be used to reduce the width of paragraphs for many design or editorial reasons.

①   Select a paragraph or paragraphs using one of the methods
previously described.

②   Choose Formats... in the Style menu. The Paragraph
Formats dialog box will be displayed.

③   Enter a value in the Left and/or Right Indent fields.

④   Click Apply to see the effect. Click OK to implement the
settings.

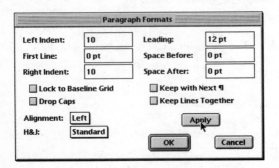

▲ When entering indents, where possible enter multiples or fractions of the font size in points: For example, if the text font size is 12 pt, choose say 12 pt, 6 pt or 18 pt.

Creating hanging indents

Hanging indents are used for listing work, where numbers, letters or bullet points occupy a space to the left of the main bulk of the text to which they refer.

① Select a paragraph or paragraphs using one of the methods previously described.

② Choose Formats... in the Style menu. The Paragraph Formats dialog box will be displayed.

③ Enter a value in the Left Indent field (such as 20 pt) and a negative value in First Line field (such as –20 pt).

④ Click Apply to see the effect. Click OK to implement the settings.

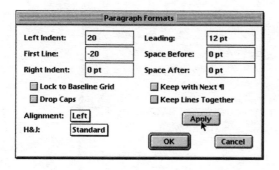

▲ The left indent acts as the initial tab in the first line of text.

You can create character-based hanging indents by inserting Command-I in the first line of a paragraph. The text in the second line will automatically align. This technique is a poor alternative to paragraph formatting.

Inserting drop caps

Drop caps give strong typographic emphasis to a paragraph start, especially the first paragraph in a story.

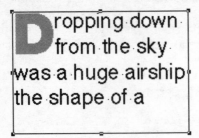

① Select a paragraph or paragraphs using one of the methods previously described.

② Choose Formats… in the Style menu. The Paragraph Formats dialog box will be displayed.

③ Check Drop caps and enter the number of characters you wish to drop (usually 1) in the Character Count field, and the number of lines you wish the dropped capital to fall in the Line Count field.

④ Click Apply to see the effect. Click OK to implement the settings.

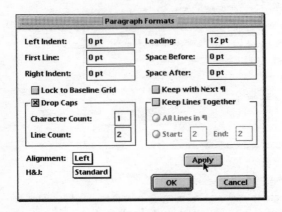

Further formatting

Inserting spaces between paragraphs

Use inter-paragraph spacing to reduce typographic density and to create visual pauses between paragraphs. You can also use spaces between paragraphs as an alternative to first line indents.

Inserting paragraph spaces

① First remove any empty paragraphs (i.e. double ¶ symbols) from your text, either by positioning the insertion point within each empty paragraph and pressing [Delete] or by using the Find/Change method.

② Select a paragraph or paragraphs using one of the methods previously described.

③ Choose Formats… in the Style menu. The Paragraph Formats dialog box will be displayed.

④ Enter amounts in the Space Before and/or Space After fields.

⑤ Click Apply to see the effect. Click OK to implement the settings.

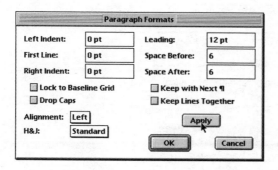

▲ When deciding which paragraphs should contain paragraph space settings, bear the following in mind.

(a) Imagine if the paragraph were to be cut and pasted elsewhere in the text. If you wish the spaces to move with the paragraph, then apply the settings within the paragraph. If you wish the spaces to remain in place, apply the settings within the adjacent paragraph(s).

(b) Be consistent when applying spaces: for instance, if the above guide does not help you to decide which paragraph should contain the settings, always apply a Space Before within the paragraph below the space.

When entering spaces before and after paragraphs, where possible enter multiples or fractions of the text leading value in points: For example, if the leading is 15 pt, choose say 10 pt, 7.5 pt or 5 pt.

✦ Leading is introduced above each line and so a very large leading value will have the effect of visually increasing the space before a paragraph. Neither leading nor paragraph spaces come into force before the first line in a text box.

Inserting rules between paragraphs

Use paragraph rules to separate lines of text visually, to underline a heading or to create a black panel under a line of white text.

Unlike rules created with the line tools, paragraph rules flow with the paragraphs when you edit or style text.

The most crucial rule attribute is offset, the distance rules are positioned above or below the paragraphs to which they belong. Unless a suitable value is entered, rules will align on or be positioned near the nearest baseline of type.

Tidy your desk when you have finished working. ¶

Switch of the lights when you leave the room.

A rule below a paragraph separating
lines of text

Ruling planets¶

Some heavenly bodies have an apparent motion of their own.

A wide 'rule above' underlying the heading
to which it's applied. Baseline Shift has been
applied to the heading to raise it a few points.

Accessing the Paragraph Rules dialog box

① Select a paragraph or paragraphs using one of the methods previously described.

② Choose Rules... in the Style menu. The Paragraph Rules dialog box will be displayed.

③ Check the Rule Below and/or Rule Above boxes.

Specifying rules

① Enter an offset value as either a percentage or points value, such as 50% or 14pt.

② Choose Indents in the Length pop-up menu, unless you wish the rule to be the same length as your text.

③ Specify other attributes as required.

④ Click Apply to see the effect. Click OK to implement the settings.

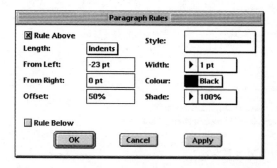

+ A percentage offset sets a proportional distance between a paragraph and an adjacent paragraph. If there is no adjacent paragraph, the rule will not be employed; if paragraph spaces are subsequently added or altered the rule will self adjust.

An offset specified in points sets a fixed distance between the upper/lower baseline of a paragraph and a rule. If the rule is at the top of a text box, the text will be lowered to accommodate the rule.

Indented rules run the width of the paragraph. If you wish rules to run the full width of a text box, enter a negative value in the From Left or From Right fields to match the *existing* paragraph indents values.

Keeping subheads with paragraphs

Headings in text should ideally remain with the paragraphs to which they refer. Otherwise you can spend a great deal of time reuniting paragraphs. You can set up your paragraph formats to do this automatically.

Top: sub-head separated from the paragraph to which it refers. *Above:* re-united sub-head.

Keeping paragraphs together

① With the Content tool active, select a paragraph or paragraphs.

② Choose Formats... in the Style menu. The Paragraph Formats dialog box will be displayed.

③ Check the Keep with Next ¶ box.

④ Click OK.

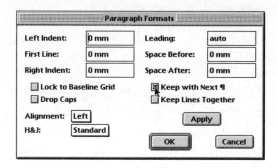

Spacing words

You can alter word and character spaces to improve the design, copyfitting, legibility or readability of text. The control within QuarkXPress is called Tracking and is measured in percentages of an en space (roughly the width of a lower-case n.) Untracked letter and character spaces are set at 0.

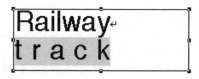

The lower word has been 'tracked' for visual effect.

① Select the text to be tracked using one of the methods previously described.

② Choose Track… in the Style menu and enter a figure in the Track dialog box.
A positive figure, such as 5 will widen the spacing; a negative figure such as –5 will tighten the spacing.

▲ When tracking text for other than design reasons, apply tracking to complete lines or, even better, complete paragraphs and use the minimum setting possible. Then tracking won't be too obvious to the reader.

Matching paragraph formatting

You can give a paragraph the same leading and alignment as another paragraph without resorting to the Style menu or Measurements palette. Both paragraphs however must be in the same text box or within linked text boxes for this technique to work.

① Position the insertion point somewhere within the paragraph you wish to style.

② Hold down [Alt]+[Shift] and click somewhere within the paragraph whose styles you wish to copy.

✦ Only paragraph formats will be copied (not character styles), unless the copied paragraph has been styled using a Style Sheet, in which case the recipient paragraph is fully restyled to match the copied paragraph's Style Sheet.

Formatting tables

Creating a simple table of contents

You can create a table of contents without needing to resort to complex tabbing or formatting by simply combining right alignment with the use of a single default tab.

What·is·design·management?→	4
Design·management:·A·neglected·discipline→	5
Three·areas·of·design·which·need·management→	7

① Type each line of text using the tab key to separate the text from the page numbers. End each line with a return.

② Select all the paragraphs using one of the methods previously described.

③ Choose Right in the Alignment sub-menu in the Style menu.

Creating multi-column tables

Multi-column tables are created by applying bespoke tab positions to individual paragraphs within tabbed text. These bespoke tabs override the default 0.5 inch tab positions which are left aligned.

The Tab key is used to insert tabs within text. These can either be inserted within a WP document before it is imported into QuarkXPress or within QuarkXPress itself.

The Paragraph Tabs dialog box is used to create new tab positions to any one of six different styles of column alignment.

It's important to remember that tabbing is a paragraph attribute; therefore any paragraph can have its own tab positions and alignments. Because of this, always try to avoid merging tabbed paragraphs accidently as your formatting may go awry.

Tabbed text with and without invisibles showing.

▲   When preparing text for tabbing, reduce the number of paragraphs within a table to the minimum. Use Shift-Returns to separate lines and use Returns only to separate those lines between which you wish to insert paragraph spaces, rules or different tabbing. Always avoid having tabs at end of lines with text wrapping from line to line.

Accessing the Paragraph Tabs dialog box

① Select a paragraph or paragraphs within the table using one of the methods previously described.

② Choose Tabs… in the Style menu. The Paragraph Tabs dialog box will be displayed together with a ruler attached to the top of the text box.

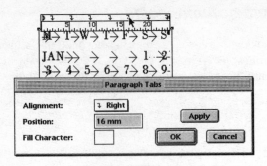

Setting new tab positions

① Select an option in the Alignment pop-up menu.

② Either: click the tab ruler above the text box to position a new tab.

 Or: enter in a value in the position field.

③ Whichever way you choose to position a new tab, click Apply to see the result. If the tab is incorrectly positioned, click-drag its icon to a new position on the ruler and click Apply again.

④ Repeat stages 1–3 until all the tabs have been inserted and correctly positioned.

⑤ Click OK.

▲ If the end of the tab ruler is off-screen, create a new tab and click-drag it right off the ruler and rest it on the edge of the document window. The window will scroll to bring the end of the ruler into view.

✦ As new tabs are applied, all the unseen default tabs to the left of the new tabs(s) are automatically removed.

Removing tabs within the Paragraph Tabs dialog box

① Either: click-drag a tab off the edge of tab ruler.

 Or: hold down [Alt] and click the tab ruler to remove all tabs.

② Replace tabs, if required, and click OK.

▲ To fill the space between tabbed copy with dots (or any other character): select the tab to the right of the proposed fill, enter a full point in the Fill box.

Adjusting the baseline position of text

Text can be moved up or down relative to its normal position within a paragraph. The control which governs its position is called Baseline Shift. Baseline Shift is similar to the Superscript/Subscript typestyle but is user definable. It can be used to 'cheat' the leading – to move parts of paragraphs up or down, when the required effect can't be achieved through leading adjustment. It also provides a means of moving a line of text up or down within a shallow text box as an alternative or supplement to vertical alignment. See *Altering the alignment of text within text boxes* (page 73).

①   Select the text to be shifted using one of the methods described under *Selecting text*.

②   Choose Baseline Shift… in the Style menu. The Baseline Shift dialog box will be displayed.

③   Enter a value, up to three times the font size.

④   Click OK.

Incremental type adjustment

The following keystroke short-cuts are useful for setting font, leading and tracking in large headings.

Altering font sizes incrementally

●   Increase font size by preset increments: ⌘ Shift + →

●   Decrease font size by preset increments: ⌘ Shift + ←

●   Press Alt for 1pt increments

Altering type sizes proportionally when scaling text box

●   Increase the font size of all the text: hold down the ⌘ Alt + Shift keys and click-drag a corner handle of the text box.

●   Alter the proportions of all the text in a text box: hold down the ⌘ key and click-drag a corner handle of the text box.

Altering type leading incrementally

- Increase by 1pt increments: ⌘ Shift + " ' .
- Decrease by 1pt increments: ⌘ Alt Shift + : .
- Press Alt for .1pt increments.

Altering kerning/tracking incrementally

- Increase by .1 en increments: ⌘ Shift + }]
- Decrease by .1 en increments: ⌘ Shift + { [
- Press Alt for .01 en increments

——— Style sheets ———

Formatting efficiently

For design consistency, many of the paragraphs in your documents should share the same formatting. For example, within a single document, all your headings should look alike, all your sub-headings should look alike, and so on.

Using style sheets enables you to set the overall formatting of paragraphs and apply consistent formatting efficiently and accurately.

Because paragraphs in QuarkXPress are a fundamental styling unit when it comes to using style sheets, you should take this into account when breaking text into paragraphs.

As a rule, all the text in a document should be formatted using style sheets, apart from master page items and those paragraphs with one-off formatting.

Try to use style sheets as much as possible in your work and don't worry if you don't get their settings right first time. They can always be amended at any time; any amendments will be automatically made to the paragraphs to which the style sheets have been applied.

Creating style sheets

Any paragraph formatted using the Style menu or Measurement palette, can provide the settings for a style sheet. This method of creating style sheets is described here.

Creating a style sheet from a sample paragraph

①   Position the insertion point somewhere within the sample paragraph.

②   Choose Style Sheets… in the Edit menu or hold down ⌘ and click on any style sheet name in Style Sheets palette. The Style Sheets dialog box will be displayed.

③   Click New. The Edit Style Sheet dialog box will be displayed.

④   Enter a name for the new style sheet in the Name field.

⑤   Click the pointer in the Keyboard Equivalent field and press a number from the numeric key pad on the keyboard. This step is optional.

⑥   Click OK. The new style sheet will now be listed in the Style Sheets listing.

⑦   Click Save.

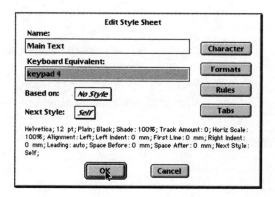

▲   A style sheet's name can describe a paragraph's function, such as 'Table Heading' or describe its specification, such as 'Times 12pt, Space After'. Numbered names, such as '1 Heading' will be numerically ordered in the Style Sheet sub-menu and Style Sheet palette. Others will appear alphabetically.

Applying style sheets

Once style sheets have been made, they can be applied to paragraphs using one of three methods:

● using the Style menu
● using the Style palette
● using the keypad

Applying style sheets using the Style menu

① Select a paragraph or paragraphs using one of the methods previously described.

② Choose a style sheet in the Style Sheets sub-menu in Style menu.

Applying style sheets using the Style palette

① Select a paragraph or paragraphs using one of the methods previously described.

② Choose Show Style Sheets in the View menu to display the Style Sheets palette.

③ Click on a style sheet name in the palette. Use the palette scroll bars if the name of the style sheet is out of view.

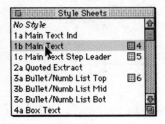

Applying style sheets using the keypad

① Select a paragraph or paragraphs using one of the methods previously described.

② Press the appropriate number in the numeric keypad.

! This method can only be used if a Keyboard Equivalent is entered in the Edit Style Sheet dialog box.

! Paragraphs that provide the specification for a style sheet are not automatically under the influence of the style sheet, although they will look correct. Ensure you apply style sheets to these paragraphs as well.

Adding further formatting to paragraphs

You can apply further formatting to any paragraph formatted by a style sheet. Such local formatting can include both character and paragraph attributes and is applied using the Style menu or Measurements palette in the usual way.

A + sign after the name of a style sheet within the Style Sheets palette indicates that further formatting has been applied. This + sign will only show if the insertion point is positioned within the locally formatted part of the text or if the whole of the paragraph is highlighted.

If another style sheet is applied to a paragraph which already has local formatting, all the local formatting will normally be retained, unless you hold down [Alt] when the new style sheet is selected within the palette.

Basing style sheets on existing style sheets

You can base a style sheet on another existing style sheet for design consistency and to speed your work. For instance, the style sheet for an italicised version of your main text can be based on the style sheet for your main text. One major advantage of basing new style sheets on existing style sheets is that if you wish to change the original style sheet, all the style sheets which are based on it automatically change as well.

① Choose Style Sheets… in the Edit menu or hold down ⌘ and click on the name of the style sheet in Style Sheets palette. The Style Sheets dialog box will be displayed.

② Click New. The Edit Style Sheet dialog box will be displayed.

③ Choose the style sheet on which you wish to base the new style sheet in the Based on pop-up menu. Enter a name for the style sheet in the Name field.

④ Click Character, Formats, Rules or Tabs to access their respective dialog boxes.

⑤ Make any changes within the dialog boxes in the usual way. Click OK to close each box. Notice the revised description of the style sheet at the bottom of the appropriate dialog box.

⑥ Click OK again to return to the Style Sheets dialog box.

⑦ Click Save.

Amending style sheets

① Choose Style Sheets… in the Edit menu or hold down ⌘ and click on the style sheet name in Style Sheets palette. The Style Sheets dialog box will be displayed.

② Click on the name of the style sheet to be edited (if it is not already selected) and click Edit.

③ Click Character, Formats, Rules or Tabs to access their respective dialog boxes.

④ Make any changes within the dialog boxes in the usual way. Click OK to close each box, click OK again to return to the Style Sheets dialog box.

⑤ Click Save.

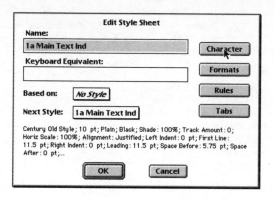

Copying Style Sheets from other documents

Style sheets you create and use in one document can be copied into other documents. Provided the names of copied style sheets do not clash with the names of existing style sheets, the process is fairly straightforward.

Either:

① Choose Style Sheets... in the Edit menu or hold down ⌘ and click on the name of any style sheet in Style Sheets palette. The Style Sheets dialog box will be displayed.

② Click Append. Use the directory dialog box controls to locate the QuarkXPress document containing the style sheets you wish to copy.

③ Click Open. The style sheets will be added to the list within the dialog box.

④ Click OK and click Save.

Or:

● Copy and paste a paragraph under the influence of the style sheet you wish to copy from one document to another, using the Apple Clipboard. See *Moving and copying text using the Clipboard* (page 41).

❗ If H&J settings (see page 140) differ between documents, it's necessary to copy the H&Js from the document containing the style sheets first. The process is similar to copying style sheets except the Append button is accessed in the H&Js for... dialog box.

Disconnecting style sheets

You can unlink a style sheet from a paragraph, yet retain its formatting. Do this if you're happy with the formatting of a paragraph but don't wish it to be effected by any future style sheet amendments. Also do this if you wish to copy a paragraph from another document, and you don't wish its style sheet to copied along with it.

● Apply No Style by one of the methods described previously.

Summary

● **Text is formatted at either a character or paragraph level.**

● **Word and character spacing is controlled locally by Tracking.**

● **Most paragraph attributes are applied within the Paragraph Formats dialog box.**

● **Simple contents tables can be created without special tabbing.**

● **Style sheets enable you to apply formatting efficiently, accurately and consistently.**

7

WORKING WITH TEXT BOXES

This chapter covers:

- the Item menu
- the Text Box Specification dialog box
- the Runaround Specifications dialog box
- the Frame Specifications dialog box
- the Measurements palette

The adept use of text boxes provides the key to effective page layout. In addition to defining simple text areas, text boxes can be divided into multiple columns, linked together, layered to create interesting type effects, and given coloured backgrounds and borders. In a sense, text boxes are like miniature pages with their own internal and external attributes.

—— Altering the layout of boxes ——

Creating multi-columned text boxes

You can easily divide the text area within text boxes into multiple linked columns. This feature is particularly useful when you wish to create a text area with a common coloured background, with or without a border.

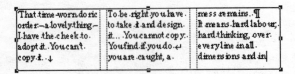

Adding extra columns to a text box

① With either the Item tool or Content tool active, select a text box.

② Choose Modify… in the Item menu. The Text Box Specifications dialog box will be displayed.

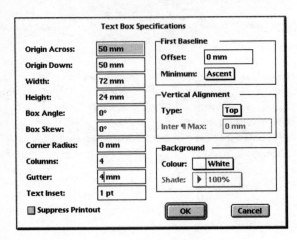

③ Enter a value in the Columns field and a value in the Gutter field.

④ Click OK.

⑤ Enter text into the text box. Provided sufficient text is entered, the text will automatically flow from one column to the next column.

▲ You can force text into the next column by positioning the insertion point before the text you wish to move and pressing the Enter key.

Altering margins within text boxes

You may wish to move text away from the inner edge of a text box for a number of reasons.

● to create a margin between a box frame and the edge of text

● to create a space above the first line of text, unattainable through paragraph formatting

● to create a text margin within a coloured box

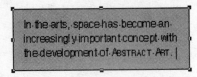

The control which governs the margins within a text box is called Text Inset. The default text inset is 1 pt and it applies to all four sides of a text box.

The control which governs the distance of the first baseline of text from the top edge of a box (or the inner edge of a frame) is called First Baseline.

Widening the inner margins

① With either the Item tool or Content tool active, select a text box.

② Choose Modify… in the Item menu. The Text Box Specifications dialog box will be displayed. Enter a value in the Text Inset field.

③ Click OK.

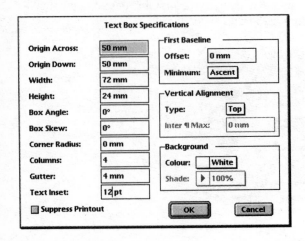

Lowering the position of the first baseline of text

① With either the Item tool or Content tool active, select a text box.

② Choose Modify... in the Item menu. The Text Box Specifications dialog box will be displayed.

③ Enter a value equal to or larger than the font size in the First Baseline, Offset field.

④ Click OK.

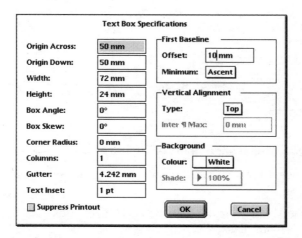

Altering the alignment of text within text boxes

Text within a text box is normally aligned to the top of a box. You can align text to the bottom of a box; this option is useful for text boxes containing footnotes.

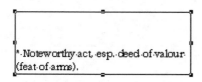

You can also range text from the centre of a text box giving equal space above and below; this option is especially useful when positioning text, such as headings and quotations, in coloured text boxes.

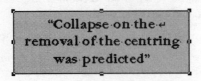

Finally you can justify text vertically; this option overrides leading settings, spacing out the lines of text to fill the depth of a text box.

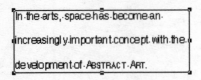

Altering the vertical alignment

① With either the Item tool or Content tool active, select a text box.

② Choose Modify... in the Item menu. The Text Box Specifications dialog box will be displayed.

③ Choose an option in the Vertical Alignment, Type pop-up menu.

④ Click OK.

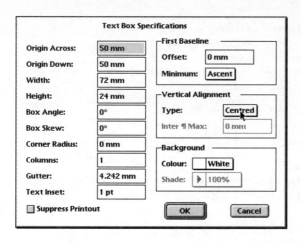

✦ Vertical Alignment Justified is often used to 'stretch out' lines to fill a text box in the absence of sufficient text. The consequential widening of space between the line alters the look of text and for this reason you may prefer to avoid this technique. Any increase in leading can be minimised by entering a value, such as 3 mm, in the Inter ¶ Max field below the Type pop-up menu when Justified is chosen.

— Overlapping and linking boxes —

Layering text

You can overlay text to create typographic effects with a sense of depth.

Normally when a text box is placed above another text box, text in the underlying box is displaced. The control which causes this effect is called Runaround and it needs to be disabled for the text to remain in place.

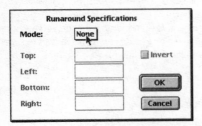

① With either the Item tool or Content tool active, select the overlying text box.

② Choose Runaround… in the Item menu. The Runaround dialog box will be displayed.

③ Choose None in the Mode pop-up menu.

④ Click OK.

Runaround Specifications

Mode: None

Top: ☐ Invert

Left:

Bottom: OK

Right: Cancel

+ Text boxes with the Runaround mode set to None will automatically become transparent if the box had previously a 0% shaded or White background.

Moving text boxes in front of/ behind each other

All items, including text boxes, have a stacking order. Older items always underlap newer items when you position them together. You can alter the stacking order at any time for either access or layout purposes.

Changing the stacking order of boxes

① With either the Item tool or Content tool active, select the text box to be moved.

② Choose Send to Back or Bring to Front in the Item menu.

▲ Hold down the Alt key when you pull down the Item menu for the additional commands Send Backward and Bring Forward.

Linking text boxes

You can link any number of text boxes together so that text flows from box to box. Linking is particularly useful when text runs across many columns and you wish to keep the text in one piece for ease of editing.

The process of linking is straightforward provided you take care only to click within the text boxes you intend to link and that you click the boxes in the order you wish the text to flow.

Linking two text boxes

① Select the Linking tool in the Tools palette.

② Move the pointer over the first text box and click once and then move the pointer over the second text box and click once again.

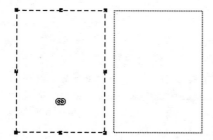

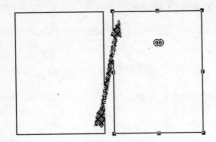

Unlinking two text boxes

① With either the Item tool or Content tool active, select one of the linked text boxes.

② Select the Unlinking tool in the Tools palette. An arrow will be displayed linking one box to the next.

③ Move the pointer over the tailfeather of the arrow and click once.

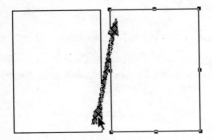

Linking more than two text boxes at a time

① Hold down Alt and select the Linking tool in the Tools palette. Release Alt and the mouse button.

② Move the pointer over the first text box and click once, move the pointer over the second text box and click once again, move the pointer over the third text box and click once again and so on.

③ Turn off the Linking tool by selecting the Item or Content tool.

Unlinking more than two text boxes at a time

① With either the Item tool or Content active, select one of the linked text boxes.

② Hold down [Alt] and select the Unlinking tool in the Tools palette. Release [Alt] and the mouse button. Arrows will be displayed linking the boxes together.

③ Move the pointer over the tailfeather of the final arrow and click once, move the pointer over the tailfeather of the arrow before it and click once again and so on.

Re-routing text

① Hold down [Alt] and select the Linking tool in the Tools palette. Release [Alt] and the mouse button.

② Move the pointer over the text box from which you wish to re-route the text and click once, move the pointer over the text box to which you wish to route the text and click once again, move the pointer over the next text box and click once again and so on.

③ Turn off the Linking tool by selecting the Item tool or Content tool.

✦ You will notice in the previous steps that the Alt key is used for multiple linkages. The role of the Alt key is to keep the Linking and Unlinking tools active. If this key is used, it is important to select the Item or Content tool immediately after you have completed the process to turn either tool off.

— Colouring and framing text boxes —

Colouring text boxes

You can give text boxes coloured backgrounds so that text areas are 'panelled'.

① With the Item tool or Content tool active, select a box.

② Choose Modify... in the Item menu. The Text Box Specifications dialog box will be displayed.

③ Choose an option in the Colour and/or Shade pop-up menus as required.

④ Click OK.

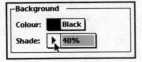

▲ Specify a text inset to create a margin between text and the edge of a coloured box to improve its appearance.

Framing text boxes

You can give text borders for emphasis and for defining text areas. These borders, or box rules, are called Frames.

Framing text boxes

① With either the Item tool or Content tool active, select a text box.

② Choose Frame… in the Item menu. The Frame Specifications dialog box will be displayed.

③ Choose a frame in the Style window and enter a value, other than 0, in the Width field. Select a Colour and/or Shade attribute as required.

④ Click OK.

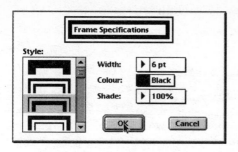

▲   Specify a text inset to create a margin between text and the edge of a framed box to improve its appearance.

—— Transforming text boxes ——

Rotating text boxes

You can rotate text to give either vertical or diagonal emphasis to a page layout.

Rotating a text box by specifying an angle

①   With either the Item tool or Content tool active, select a text box.

②   Enter a value in the Box Angle field in the Measurements palette. Press `Enter ↵`.

❗   When specifying rotation angles for large items or items positioned near the edge of a page, it is necessary to allow for sufficient rotation space. Move an item into the centre of the page first, rotate the item and then reposition it.

✚   Items rotated by entering a value are rotated about the item's centre-point.

Rotating a text box using the Rotation tool

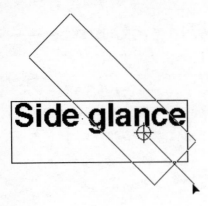

①   With either the Item tool or Content tool active, select a text box.

②   Select the Rotation tool in the Tool palette and click at the point of rotation and, without releasing the mouse button, drag away from the point to create a 'lever'; follow it with a movement in a clockwise or anti-clockwise direction.

③   Release the mouse button.

▲   Hold down the Shift key when using the Rotation tool to rotate in 45° increments.

Skewing text boxes

You can skew text for visual effect.

①   With either the Item tool or Content tool active, select a text box.

②   Choose Modify... in the Item menu.The Text Box Specifications dialog box will be displayed.

③   Enter a value in the Box Skew field.

④   Click OK.

Flipping text boxes

You can flip text horizontally and/or vertically for special effect.

①   With either the Item tool or Content tool active, select a text box.

Either:

②   choose Flip Horizontal or Vertical in the Style menu.

Or:

②   click on the Horizontal or Vertical arrow icons in the middle of the Measurements palette.

Summary

● The adept use of text boxes provides the key to effective page layout.

● Text boxes have both internal and external attributes.

● Linked and multi-column text boxes enable long pieces of text to be kept together for ease of editing.

● Coloured and framed text boxes require an appropriate text inset.

● Disabling Runaround enables text to be overlaid to give depth to a layout.

8

ADDING HEADERS AND PAGE NUMBERS

This chapter covers:

- the Document Layout palette
- master pages
- the Section dialog box

—————— Using master pages ——————

In multi-page documents, there is likely to be some text that appears on all or most pages; headers (running heads), footers and page numbers are typical examples of such items. Fortunately there is no need for you to enter such items on every page. To do so would be time-consuming and inconsistencies will inevitably creep in however carefully you worked.

The easiest way to enter such items, and to ensure consistency, is to use master pages. The default master page is Master A and its icon can be viewed in the Document Layout palette.

Master A already provides each document page with the blue margin and column guides. Place items at any time on this master page and they will automatically be copied onto document pages as if you had created them on each page individually.

You can modify master page items on a document page without affecting the originals on the master page itself.

Adding master page items

Opening Master A

① Choose Document Layout in the View menu.

② Double-click the icon to the left of A-Master A. Master A will then be displayed. A broken Link icon at the top left of a page indicates the page is a master page.

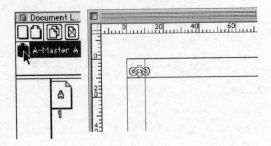

+ In the case of Facing Page documents, Master A comprises both left and right-hand pages.

Adding headers and footers within Master A

① Create text boxes in the top and bottom margin areas (on both left and right-hand pages in the case of a Facing Pages document).

② Enter text and format in the usual way.

Closing Master A

Either:

● choose Document in the Display sub-menu in the Page menu.

Or:

● double-click any document page in the Document Layout palette.

▲ Because master page items appear on all pages of your document, ensure they are accurately placed and formatted. Provided you do not alter the items locally on individual document pages, you can always return to the items on Master A and make alterations and these alterations will be reproduced on all document pages.

You can re-apply master page items to individual document pages, by click-dragging the A-Master A icon over a document page icon in the Document Layout palette. Altered items on a page will be kept or deleted depending on the setting in the Master Page Items pop-up menu in the General Preferences dialog box.

———— Page numbering ————

Managing page numbers

By default, page numbers in QuarkXPress follow the order of the pages in the Document Layout palette. Thus the third page of the document will be labelled Page 3 at the bottom of the document window and numbered 3 on the document page itself (should a page number code be present).

You can alter the page numbering at any time to meet your editorial needs. When you do this, the new page numbers which appear on document pages and at the bottom of the document window may differ from the page numbers shown in the Document Layout palette. This is quite normal. The Document Layout palette always shows the 'absolute' page numbers, however you have numbered your pages.

Page numbering sequences (called Sections in QuarkXPress) can start on any document page. Each section can have a different numbering format from a choice of Roman and Arabic characters.

Bear in mind that section start numbers must be even on left-hand pages and odd on right-hand pages in Facing Pages documents. Otherwise the first page in a section will automatically move to the correct side of the document's spine.

Adding page numbers within Master A

① Open A-Master A as shown previously.

② Create text boxes in the top, bottom or side margin areas (on both left and right-hand pages in the case of a Facing Pages document).

③ Within the text box(s) press ⌘ + #3. The page number code <#> will appear. Format the code as you would format normal text.

④ Double-click on any document page icon on the Document Layout palette to return to the document pages. The page number will be present and correct for each page.

Restarting page number sequences

① Choose Document Layout in the View menu.

② Double-click the page at which you wish the page numbering to restart.

③ Choose Section… in the Page menu. The Section dialog box will be displayed.

④ Click to check the Section Start box.

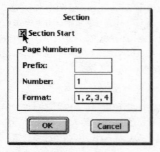

⑤ Enter a number in the Number field or leave it as 1.

⑥ Choose a style of Arabic or Roman numbering in the Format pop-up menu.

⑦ Click OK. An asterisk will appear on the page icon in the Document Layout palette indicating a section start.

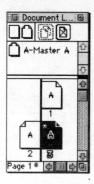

—— **Adding other master pages** ——

Creating additional master pages

① Choose Document Layout in the View menu.

② Click-drag the Blank Facing Pages icon (second icon, top row) to within the same window as Master A. (In the case of a non-facing pages document, use the Blank Single Page icon.)

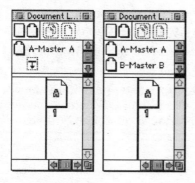

③ Double-click the new icon to the left of Master B. Master B will then be displayed. A broken Link icon at the top left of a page indicates the page is a master page.

④ Choose Master Guides... in the Page menu.

⑤ Enter new values in the Master guides and Column guides fields, as required.

⑥ Click OK.

⑦ Choose Document in the Display sub-menu in the Page menu.

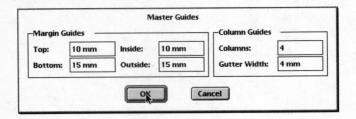

Summary

● Repeated items, such as headers, footers and page numbers, can be placed on master pages.

● Items placed on master pages are automatically copied onto document pages.

● A special page number code provides the correct page number for each document page.

● Documents can contain different page numbering sequences.

● Provided you do not alter master page items locally on document pages, alterations to master page items are automatically reproduced on document pages.

9

WORKING WITH ITEMS

This chapter covers:

- the Item tool and menu
- the Apple Clipboard
- anchored boxes
- box shapes and polygons
- the Space/Align dialog box

– Selecting and manipulating items –

Items are normally selected with the Item tool and item attributes
are applied through the Item menu. You can use the Content tool to
select and alter the dimensions of individual items. The Item tool
must be selected, however, when you move or copy items using the
Apple Clipboard, otherwise an item's content will be moved or
copied instead of the item itself.

Selecting and deselecting items

Selecting multiple items

① With the Item tool active, click on the first item.

② Hold down ⌗Shift and click on other items to be selected.

▲ Clicking an item a second time when the Shift key is held down will deselect an item, a third time reselect an item and so on.

Selecting multiple items by marqueeing

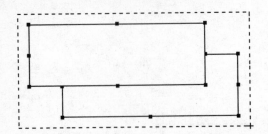

● With the Item tool active, click-drag from a point on the blank area of the page diagonally across all the items to be selected.

Selecting all items on a spread

● With the Item tool active, choose Select All in the Edit menu.

Deselecting all items on a spread

Either:

● click a blank part of a page.

Or:

● with the Item tool active, press ⌗Tab.

Selecting underlying items

① With the Item tool or Content tool active, hold down ⌘ Alt Shift and click on the overlying item.

② Click once more to select the item immediately underneath.

③ Click once again to select a further underlying item and so on.

④ Release all keys.

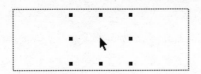

Positioning and sizing items accurately

①   With the Item tool active, select an item or items.

②   Enter values in the X, Y, W and H fields in the measurements palette. Press [Enter ↵]

Locking items in position

Very small or large items can be locked to a page so they cannot be moved accidentally through the use of the mouse.

①   With the Item tool active, select an item or items.

②   Choose Lock in the Item menu. A padlock icon will appear if you try to move or resize the item.

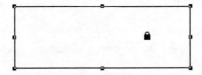

✚   Locked items can be moved by the cursor keys only and are *not* protected from accidental deletion.

Duplicating items

① With the Item tool active, select an item or items.

② Choose Duplicate in the Item menu. The duplicate will be offset from the original item(s).

Grouping items together

Related items, such as logotypes and straplines, can be grouped so that they act as a single entity while the Item tool is selected.

Grouping items

① With the Item tool active, select the items you wish to group.

② Choose Group in the Item menu. A dotted border will appear when a group is selected with the Item tool.

✦ You can modify items within a group with the Content tool active.

Moving items in front of/behind each other

All items have a stacking order. Older items always underlap newer items when positioned together. You can alter the stacking order at any time for either access or layout purposes.

Changing the stacking order of items

① With the Item tool active, select the item to be moved.

② Choose Send to Back or Bring to Front in the Item menu.

▲ Hold down the Alt key when you pull down the Item menu for the additional commands Send Backward and Bring Forward.

Moving and copying items using the Clipboard

Items are either moved or copied from page to page or from document to document using the Apple Clipboard (a short term storage area assigned for this purpose). Any item which you cut or copy is automatically placed on the Clipboard.

However many times you paste, the item will remain on the Clipboard until another item is cut or copied.

▲ The current contents of the Clipboard can be viewed at any time by choosing View Clipboard in the Edit menu.

Moving items elsewhere

① With the Item tool active, select the item or items you wish to move, by using one of the methods described previously. Choose Cut in the Edit menu.

② Move to the page where you wish to move the item and choose Paste in the Edit menu. The item will be pasted in the centre of the document window.

Copying items elsewhere

① With the Item tool active, select the item or items you wish to copy. Choose Copy in the Edit menu.

② Move to the page where you wish to place the item and choose Paste in the Edit menu. The item will be pasted in the centre of the document window.

Anchored text and picture boxes

Sometimes you may wish to include a text or picture box within a text area and have it move with the text during editing work. The way you achieve this is to 'anchor' a box within the text. The process is essentially quite simple and makes use of the Apple Clipboard.

Usually, when the Clipboard is used, *either* the Content *or* Item tool is active throughout the cutting/copying and pasting process. In the case of anchored items, the *Item tool* is active when the item is cut or copied. The *Content tool* is active for the pasting stage. It's an ingenious use of the Apple Clipboard.

```
save their ships where
they laie at  Anchor  by no
cunning or shift could
```

Anchoring a box in text

①   Create a text box in the usual way, but make its height no larger than the leading of the text in which it is going to be anchored (to match the example shown).

②   Insert text into the box and then format it.

③   Select the Item tool.

④   Choose Cut or Copy in the Edit menu.

⑤   Select the Content tool.

⑥   In another text box, position the insertion point where you wish to anchor the new box within the text.

⑦   Choose Paste in the Edit menu. A three-handled text box will be anchored in the text.

▲   Use the same process to anchor picture boxes in text.

Moving an anchored box relative to the text baseline

①   With either the Content tool or Item tool active, select the anchored text box.

②   Select either alignment option at the far left of the Measurements palette.

③   In addition or alternatively, with either the Content tool or Item tool active, select the area underlying the anchored box as you would select normal text and choose Baseline Shift… in the Style menu. Enter a positive or negative value.

④   Click OK.

Adding lines and arrows

Use vertical lines (rules) to separate columns of text and horizontal lines to separate articles. Diagonal rules give layouts a dynamic quality.

① Select one of the line tools by clicking once only on its icon in the Tool palette.

② Move the mouse (without pressing the button) over the page. The pointer turns into a cross hair. Move the cross hair to where you wish one end of the line to be.

③ Click-drag (press the mouse button and move the mouse with the button depressed) to where you wish the other end of the line to be. Release the mouse button.

④ Choose attributes in the sub-menus in the Style menu.

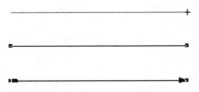

▲ Hold down the Shift key to constrain a diagonal line to 45° increments.

Creating polygons and altering box shapes

Create polygons to add unusual shapes and images to layouts. Multi-sided text boxes are useful for forcing text areas into shapes, such as when you wish text to follow shapes within an underlying image.

Creating polygons from scratch

① Select the Polygon tool in the tool palette.

② Move the mouse (without pressing the button) over the page. The pointer turns into a cross hair. Move the cross hair to where you wish the first corner point of the polygon to be. Click on the page.

③ Click again to position the next corner point. Repeat until all but the final corner point are in place.

④ Either: double-click to position the final corner point; the polygon shape will be completed for you.

Or: click to position the final corner point and then position the pointer over the very first corner point you created. A round-cornered rectangle will appear indicating you have correctly positioned the pointer. Click to complete the polygon.

Switching between standard box shapes

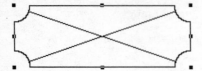

① With either the Content tool or Item tool active, select a text or picture box.

② Select an option in the Box Shape sub-menu in the Item menu.

Creating polygons from standard text and picture boxes

① With either the Content tool or Item tool active, select a text or picture box.

② Choose the Polygon option in the Box Shape sub-menu in the Item menu.

③ Choose Reshape Polygon in the Item menu (to tick the command, if it is not already ticked).

④ Reshape the item by click-dragging its handles.

▲ Hold down the Command key and click on a polygon handle to delete the handle and click on the polygon's path to add a handle.

Spacing and aligning items

You can accurately space and align items using the Space/Align controls. The controls are not particulraly intuitive; experiment with items until you fully understand the effects of each pop-up menu and radio button option.

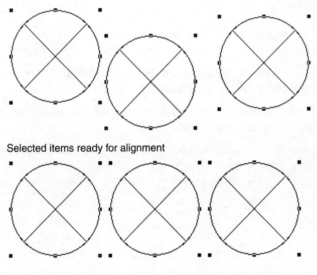

Selected items ready for alignment

Items vertically aligned and horizontally distributed

① With the Item tool active, select more than one item.

② Choose Space/Align... in the Item menu.

③ Check the Horizontal box to enter set horizontal spacing and alignments.

④ Check the Vertical box to enter set vertical spacing and alignments.

⑤ Click OK.

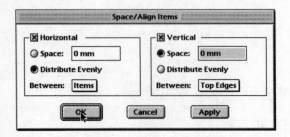

Summary

● Use the Item tool for multiple selections or for moving items with or without the Apple Clipboard.

● Lock items which are small or very large so they can't be moved accidently.

● Group items together if their spatial relationship needs to be maintained.

● Use the Content tool for selecting and manipulating text, images and boxes within groups.

10

IMPORTING IMAGES

This chapter covers:

- picture boxes
- picture entry options
- the Apple Clipboard
- file formats
- the Library palette
- the Style menu
- the Runaround dialog box
- the Frame dialog box
- the Picture Box Specifications dialog box

—— Working with picture boxes ——

Picture boxes within QuarkXPress are the equivalent to the pasted-down photographs or drawn picture rectangles used in conventional artwork. You place images in these boxes which you create on document pages as you work.

Picture boxes define the crop (visible area) of images; their size and position together with text boxes, determines the page layout.

They are also used without graphics to create coloured panels and borders (box rules).

Picture boxes are often aligned with margin, column or ruler guides for accurate positioning.

You can place as many picture boxes as you like on a document page. They can always be altered in size and the images within them changed.

Creating and resizing picture boxes

Creating a picture box

① Select the rectangular Picture Box tool by clicking once only on its icon in the Tool palette.

② Move the mouse (without pressing the button) over the page. The pointer turns into a cross hair. Move the cross hair to where you wish the top left of the box to be (marked A).

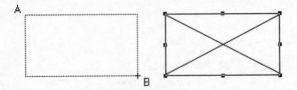

③ Click-drag (press the mouse button and move the mouse with the button depressed) diagonally to where you wish the bottom right corner of the box to be (marked B). Release the mouse button.

▲ You can use the same process to create other box shapes, except for polygons.

Resizing a picture box

① With either the Item tool or Content tool active, click once somewhere within a box (if not already selected). Move the pointer to one of the handles at the bottom of the picture box. The pointer turns into a pointing hand.

② Whilst the pointing hand is displayed, click-drag the handle downwards to resize the box.

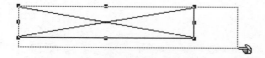

▲ Handles halfway along the side of boxes can be used to enlarge or reduce a box in one direction only. Corner handles enable you to enlarge or reduce a box in two directions at once.

Moving and deleting picture boxes

Moving a picture box or other item

● With the Item tool active, click-drag the middle of an item.

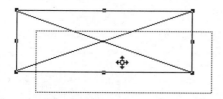

▲ To move an item whilst the Content tool is selected, hold down the Command key whilst click-dragging the item.

Deleting a picture box or other item

Either:

● with the Item tool active, press [Delete].

Or:

● with either the Item tool or Content tool active, choose Delete in the Item menu.

—— Ways of working with images ——

You can't create images directly within QuarkXPress since it's strictly a page layout program. You create vector images for illustrations and charts within specialised draw, chart and spreadsheet programs and bitmapped images within specialised paint programs or by scanning photographs.

Vector images are comprised of mathematically-described PostScript paths either drawn by users on-screen or created automatically by programs. The images are resolution-free and scalable, which makes the technology ideal for logotypes, charts and other visual devices, the sizes of which cannot be pre-determined.

Bitmapped images are mosaics of pixels, often created by scanning originals, such as photographs, and invariably manipulated by users on-screen. They have a resolution (measured in pixels per inch) which limits how much they can be rescaled.

Scanned (bitmapped) images, unlike vector images, have large file sizes which can create storage problems. Additionally, good scanning equipment is expensive and scanning is an art in itself. However, there are several strategies you can adopt if you lack sufficient storage capacity or the appropriate equipment and/or expertise. One way is to import roughly scanned, low resolution, images into your documents. These images will be good enough to work with and may be good enough to print from, and will give an indication of the treatment and positioning of images to all concerned.

After you have completed your documents, professionally scanned, high resolution versions of images can be substituted for the low resolution images, whether you are planning to imageset your documents or just wish to have the best possible printing quality. The advantage of this approach is that you avoid having to store large picture files on your system and you leave the accurate scanning work to others.

This basic idea has been incorporated into a system called OPI, a sophisticated process of image duplication and file substitution used for the imagesetting of large documents involving many images.

Another way is to import accurately scanned images from the start. If you have neither the skills nor the equipment to produce scans to the right quality, ask your bureau to carry out this work before you start the page layout process.

A final way is simply not to worry about scanning at all at the page layout stage; just create picture boxes and frame them. The printed frames indicate where the images will go and you supply your bureau with the original transparencies and prints and tell them which image goes where and how they are to be sized and cropped.

If you are working with vectored drawings and charts, no scanning is involved at all so any imported drawings and charts should print well, provided you have saved them in the appropriate file format.

Inserting images

When you import scanned and vectored images into a QuarkXPress document, low resolution bitmapped versions of the original images are embedded within the document (unless any files are in PICT format, in which case the images are embedded at full resolution). Links between embedded images and their original images are automatically made during the importing process.

When you output your documents, QuarkXPress takes the data detailing the positional, scaling and cropping of the embedded images and applies it to the original images which it uses for out-putting purposes.

You can insert images into picture boxes in many ways. One method is covered here. The use of the Apple Clipboard method is explained later in this chapter.

✚ The tonal/colour quality of embedded bitmapped images is set within the Application Preferences dialog box. Set at the lowest quality if you wish to keep your QuarkXPress file sizes as small as possible.

Importing images using Get Picture

①   With the Content tool active, select a picture box.

②   Choose Get Picture... in the File menu. The Get Picture directory dialog box will be displayed.

③   Use the directory dialog box controls to locate the picture.

④   Click Open.

Selecting images

An image is selected by clicking once on its picture box with the Content tool active.

The pointer turns into a grabber hand on the selected image.

Deleting images

●   With the Content tool active, select the picture box and press Delete .

Cropping, scaling and fitting images

Cropping pictures

① With the Content tool active, select an image.

   Either:

② click-drag the image within the picture box.

   Or:

② press ⬅, ➡, ⬇ or ⬆ to move the image in 1pt increments.

   Or:

② enter values in the X+ (pt across) and Y+ (pt vertically) fields in the Measurements palette.

   Or:

② resize the picture box.

▲ When using the Arrow keys, hold down the Alt key to move in 0.1pt increments.

Scaling images

① With the Content tool active, select an image.

Either:

② enter values in the X% (% width) and Y% (% height) fields in the Measurements palette.

Or:

② press 〔 ⌘ 〕〔 Alt 〕〔 Shift 〕 + 〔 > 〕 to increase the scale in 5% increments. Use 〔 < 〕 to decrease the scale.

Or:

② hold down 〔 ⌘ 〕〔 Alt 〕〔 Shift 〕 and click-drag a corner handle of the picture box.

! Avoid enlarging images more than 165%, as image degradation may take place when outputting.

Centring images within picture boxes

● With the Content tool active, select an image and press 〔 ⌘ 〕〔 Shift 〕 + 〔 M 〕 (for Middle) and click a corner handle of the picture box.

Fitting images within picture boxes without distortion

● With the Content tool active, select an image and press down 〔 ⌘ 〕〔 Alt 〕〔 Shift 〕 + 〔 F 〕 (for Fit).

Fitting images within picture boxes with distortion

● With the Content tool active, select the picture box and press down ⌘ Shift +F (for Fit).

! Using distorted images within a QuarkXPress document substantially increases printing and imagesetting times and can prevent a document from outputting at all. This is because the remapping of the image is implemented during the outputting process and it is demanding on processing time.

Moving and copying images using the Clipboard

Moving and copying images is normally done using the Apple Clipboard. Any images which you cut or copy are automatically placed on the Clipboard.

However many times you paste, an image will remain on the Clipboard until another image is cut or copied.

Moving images

① With the Content tool active, select the image you wish to move. Choose Cut in the Edit menu.

② Select the picture box to which you wish to move the image and choose Paste in the Edit menu.

Copying images

① With the Content tool active, select the image you wish to copy. Choose Copy in the Edit menu.

② Select the picture box to which you wish to place the copied image and choose Paste in the Edit menu.

Colouring, shading and inverting images

Line and grayscale images can be coloured and inverted (made negative) for visual effect. Line images can also be shaded.

Logo in positive   Logo made negative

Colouring images

① With the Content tool active, select the picture box.

② Choose an option in the colour and Shade sub-menus in the Style menu.

Inverting images

① With the Content tool active, select the picture box.

② Choose Negative in the Style menu.

—— Manipulating picture boxes ——

Framing picture boxes

Picture boxes can be given printed borders for emphasis and for defining picture areas. These borders (or box rules) are called Frames.

Framing picture boxes

① With either the Item tool or Content tool active, select a picture box.

② Choose Frame… in the Item menu. The Frame Specifications dialog box will be displayed.

③   Choose a frame in the Style window and enter a value, other
     than 0, in the Width field. Select a Colour and/or Shade
     attribute as required.

④   Click OK.

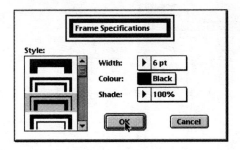

Adding borders to pages

Large picture boxes can be placed on pages and framed to give a
printed border (box rule). It can be a wise precaution to lock boxes
used for this purpose and bring guides to the front so they are showing.

If you've made the box after other items, you will need, of course, to
send the box to the back so that the other items are in front.

Framing pages

①   Create a picture box to the size of the proposed border (box
     rule).

②   Choose Frame... in the Item menu. The Frame Specifications
     dialog box will be displayed.

③   Choose a frame in the Style window and enter a value, other
     than 0, in the Width field. Select a Colour and/or Shade
     attribute as required.

④   Click OK.

⑤   Choose Send to Back in the Item menu if other page items
     have been hidden.

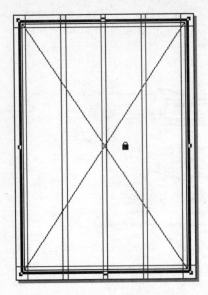

⑥   Choose General… in the Preferences sub-menu in the Edit menu. The General Preferences dialog box will be displayed.

⑦   Choose In front in the Guides pop-up menu.

⑧   Click OK.

⑨   Choose Lock in the Item menu.

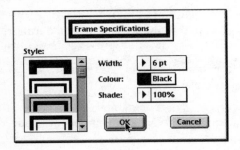

Colouring picture boxes

Picture boxes can be given coloured backgrounds to create coloured panels.

① With either the Item tool or Content tool active, select a picture box.

② Choose Modify... in the Item menu. The Picture Box Specifications dialog box will be displayed.

③ Choose an option in the Colour and/or Shade pop-up menus as required.

④ Click OK.

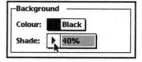

—————— Transforming images ——————

Skewing picture boxes and images

Images can be skewed within a QuarkXPress document for visual effect. This can be achieved by skewing a picture box (which effectively skews any image within it as well), by skewing the image itself (independently of the box it's within as well) or by skewing an image before importation, using an image manipulation program, such as Adobe Photoshop.

Skewing images

①   With the Content tool active, select a picture box.

Either:

②   choose Modify... in the Item menu.

③   Enter a value in the Box Skew field to skew a box together with its contents.

④   Click OK.

Or:

②   enter a value in the Skew field in the Measurements palette to skew an image independently of its box.

Rotating picture boxes

Rotating a picture box by specifying an angle

①   With either the Item tool or Content tool active, select a picture box.

②   Enter a value in the Box Angle field in the measurements palette. Press Enter ↵.

Rotating a picture box using the Rotate tool

①   With either the Item tool or Content tool active, select a picture box.

②   Select the Rotation tool in the tools palette and click at the centre point of rotation and, without releasing the mouse button, drag away from the centre point to create a 'lever'; follow it with a movement in a clockwise or anti-clockwise direction.

!   Rotating and skewing images within a QuarkXPress document substantially increases printing and imagesetting times and can prevent a document from outputting at all. This is because the remapping of the image is implemented during the outputting process and it is demanding on processing time.

▲   Hold down the Shift key when using the Rotation tool to rotate in 45° increments.

▲   When specifying rotation angles for large items or items positioned near the edge of a page, it is necessary to allow sufficient rotation space. Move an item into the centre of the page first, rotate the item and then reposition.

Flipping picture boxes

①   With either the Item tool or Content tool active, select a picture box.

Either:

②   choose Flip Horizontal or Vertical in the Style menu.

Or:

②   click on the Horizontal or Vertical arrow icons in the middle of the Measurements palette.

Running text around images

Text can run around picture boxes or the profile of images within boxes. Normally when a picture box is placed above a text box, text in the underlying box is displaced. The control which causes this effect is called Runaround.

Without further ado the spotted dog was heading back home for his dinner.

Adjusting the Runaround distance

① With either the Item tool or Content tool active, select the overlying picture box.

② Choose Runaround... in the Item menu.

③ Enter in values in the Top, Left, Bottom and Right fields as required.

④ Click OK.

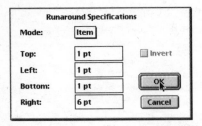

Running text around part of an image

Without further ado the spotted dog was heading back home for his dinner.

① With either the Item tool or Content tool active, select the overlying picture box.

②   Choose Runaround... in the Item menu.

③   Choose Auto Image in the Mode pop-up menu.

④   Click OK.

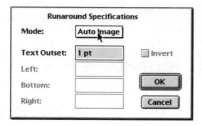

Adjusting the Runaround path

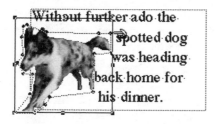

①   With either the Item tool or Content tool active, select the overlying picture box.

②   Choose Runaround... in the Item menu.

③   Choose Manual Image in the Mode pop-up menu.

④   Click OK. An editable path follows the profile of the image.

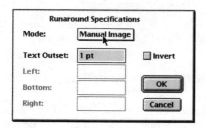

⑤ Click-drag the handles on the editable path to alter its position.

⑥ Hold down ⌘ and click on the path's handles to delete them or click on the path between handles to add new handles.

File formats

All scanned and drawn images to be imported into a document should be saved in PICT, TIFF or EPS formats.

Vectored drawings/charts and scans can be saved in PICT. This is Apple's native format and it uses the same routines as the software which draws the Macintosh screen. PICT files always embed themselves in their entirety within your document so you don't need to keep the original files with a document for output.

Scanned images are often saved in Tagged Image File Format (TIFF). This format was originally developed by Microsoft and Aldus and has become a standard worldwide. TIFF files do not embed themselves within a document so you need to keep the original files for outputting purposes.

Vectored drawn images are saved in Encapsulated PostScript (EPS), as are scanned images containing PostScript elements. This format was originally developed by Altsys, is generic and comes in many forms. Drawings produced in Macromedia FreeHand and Adobe Illustrator, for instance, are saved in this format. EPS files, like TIFF files, do not embed themselves within your document so you need to keep the original files for outputting purposes. EPS files are substantially larger than TIFFs, about a third again in size, so it's best to use TIFFs where possible for scanned images.

Specifying resolutions

Scanned images ideally should have a resolution of twice the proposed half-tone screen. If, for example, your printer will be using a 150 lpi screen, the resolution of the images should be 300 dpi (ppi).

Always ask your printer for the screen size they propose to use for your job and inform the bureau of the size before they imageset your document.

If you are scanning images for temporary use only, a resolution of 72 dpi (ppi) is fine; if you are planning to output your document on your digital printer only, check the default half-tone screen in the Page Setup dialog box and multiply the figure by 2. Make sure the correct printer is selected in the Chooser before doing this.

Specifying a file format

For scanned images, choose TIFF, unless the image contains a PostScript element, such as a clipping path, in which case choose EPS.

For drawn images, choose EPS or PICT, if EPS is not an available option.

Avoid PICT, where possible, unless you wish to apply colour to line (1-bit) or grayscale (8-bit) images within the document and you don't want to bother with linked files. Remember that they can be less reliable when outputting.

TIFF and EPS come both in PC and Macintosh versions. Macintosh versions don't work within Windows documents and vice versa.

—————— Storing images ——————

You can store items you use frequently within documents in a library for ease of access. Such items may include logos, pictures and text items. Libraries can contain grouped, locked and layered items: in fact, all QuarkXPress items whatever their attributes.

Creating a library

① Choose Library... in the New sub-menu in the File menu. The New Library directory dialog box will be displayed.

② Name the library.

③ Use the Directory dialog box controls to locate a folder in which to save the new library.

④ Click Create. The Library palette will be displayed.

Opening an existing library

① Choose Open... in the File menu. The Open dialog box will be displayed.

② Use the Directory dialog box controls to locate the library.

③ Click Open. The Library palette will be displayed.

Placing items in the library

① With the Item tool active, click-drag any item from the document into the Library palette. Park the item as indicated by the twin arrows.

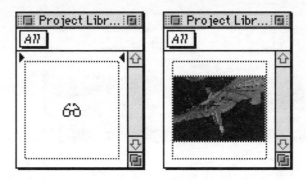

②   Double-click the parked item. The Library Entry dialog box will be displayed.

③   Name the item in the Label field. Click OK.

Taking copies from an open library

The library shows at any one time all stored items, unlabelled items or named items.

①   Choose an item in the pop-up menu in the Library palette. If the item is not listed, choose Unlabelled. The item will be displayed in the palette.

②   With either the Content tool or the Item tool selected, click-drag the item from the Library palette onto the document page.

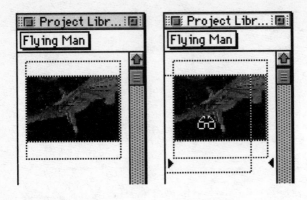

✛ Images held in the library maintain their links with original external files and these links are maintained when copies are taken from the library, as if they had been imported directly.

Summary

● Images within a document can be either vector or bitmapped.

● Use the standard 'Get Picture' method for all images.

● Avoid re-scaling bitmapped images to more than 165%.

● Images should be manipulated within an editing program rather than within QuarkXPress.

● Store regularly-used images in the library.

● Picture boxes can be used to create borders or simple graphic elements.

11

USING COLOURS

This chapter covers:

- the Edit Colours dialog box
- the Text Box Specifications dialog box
- the Picture Box Specifications dialog box
- the Frame and Paragraph Rules dialog boxes
- the Colours palette

Adding new colours

Ten basic colours already exist within a QuarkXPress document. These colours are:

- the four process colours: cyan, magenta, yellow and black (CMYK)

- the three RGB colours: red, green and blue

- white (representing white paper)

- registration (for registration and trim marks)

- none (transparent)

The CMYK colours are the process colours used by desktop printers and web offset printing machines to reproduce full colour photographs or illustrations. They are also used as a basis for creating new colours.

These colours, apart from the yellow, are a bit harsh unmixed, so don't use them individually in colouring work unless you really have to.

The RGB colours are intended for multimedia or other work confined to monitors so it is best to avoid these too.

The ten colours shown
in the Colours palette

White represents the colour of the paper you are printing on, whether it's pure white or not. Boxes, by default, have an opaque white background, so when they are placed over other items, the 'white' paper is exposed.

If you wish to print white for silkscreen purposes, create a new pale colour (any colour will do) and specify it as a spot colour. You can then inform your printer that this colour represents white and they will then use a white ink when screening the colour.

The colour described as 'none' is transparent. If boxes are given a 'none' background and placed over other items, the underlying items will show through. Don't make boxes transparent for the sake of it, as outputting times are significantly increased if you have a large number of boxes specified this way.

! Uncheck Display Correction in the Application Preferences dialog box unless you have the Efi Colour Management System set up correctly.

Adding new colours

① Choose Colours… in the Edit menu. The Colours for … dialog box will be displayed. Click New.

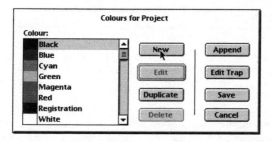

② Either: leave unchecked the Process Separations box if you wish the new colour to print as a spot colour.

Or: check the Process Separations box if you wish the colour to be reproduced using the process colours (CMYK).

If you are not sure which option to specify, move to the next step and come back to this step later.

If you are only wishing to print a document on a composite grayscale or colour printer, either setting will produce results.

③ Choose either CMYK or Pantone in the Model pop-up menu.

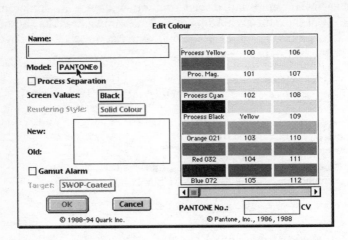

! CMYK in the Model pop-up menu refers to the colour model used for creating a colour and not to the way a colour will be reproduced by QuarkXPress.

▲ Specify spot (uncheck Process Separations) for any additional colour to black for printed matter using only two or three colours, or as an additional colour to the process colours, when a process equivalent is not accurate enough.

Specify Process Separations for all colours for printed matter with full colour pictures already using the process colours, unless a process equivalent is not accurate enough. Every spot colour in addition to the process colours will substantially increase printing costs.

✦ Spot colours are printed as a separate ink. Process separated colours are printed using the CMYK colours, whichever colour model is selected.

④ Complete the steps under the following CMYK model and Pantone model headings.

CMYK model

① Type a name in the Name field. It will not be possible for you to save a new colour unless you give it a name.

② Either: enter % values in the Cyan, Magenta, Yellow and Black fields.

Or: click-drag the sliders to the right of the % fields.

Whichever method you use, a dot will move around on the colour wheel and the colour mix will be displayed in the New panel.

③ Click OK. Click Save.

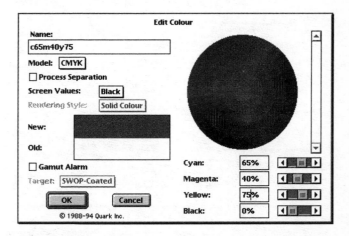

▲ When you name a CMYK colour you can give it a descriptive name, such as Poppy, or give it a name describing its composition, such as c65m40y75k0.

Always refer to a book of process colours when choosing colours, as the colours on your monitor will be misleading.

Pantone model

① Leave the Name field blank as it will be filled in automatically when you choose a colour.

② Either: click on a swatch in the window. Use the scroll bars to view the full colour range.

Or: enter a known reference number in the Pantone No. field.

The colour mix will be displayed in the New box and the name automatically entered into the Name box.

③ Click OK. Click Save.

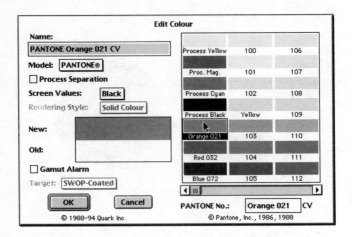

! Avoid altering a given Pantone name, unless Process Separations is checked. Otherwise any imported images using the same Pantone colour will create an additional film quite unnecessarily.

▲ Always refer to a book of Pantone colours when choosing colours as the colours on your monitor will be misleading.

✦ Pantone colours (apart from the fluorescent and metallic colours) are mixed using up to eleven basic colours. By choosing a Pantone swatch for a spot colour, you can be assured that the printer will be able to provide a true colour match.

Applying colours

You can apply colour to text, paragraph rules, lines, box backgrounds and frames, line and grayscale pictures.

Colouring paragraph rules

① Select the paragraph or paragraphs with the rules.

② Choose Rules... in the Style menu. The Paragraph Rules dialog box will be displayed.

③ Choose options in the Colour and Shade pop-up menus.

④ Click Apply to preview the colour change. Click OK to implement the colour change.

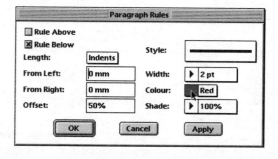

Colouring and shading box frames

You can use a drag-and-drop technique to alter the colour of box frames using the Colours palette, provided at least one box is selected. Shade adjustments however are restricted to selected boxes. Alternatively you can alter the frame colour and shade of selected boxes within the Frame Specifications dialog box.

① With either the Item tool or Content tool active, select a text or picture box.

Either:

② choose Show Colours in the View menu. The Colours palette will be displayed.

③ Click the left-hand Frame icon at the top of the palette.

④ Either: click on a colour name.

Or: click-drag a colour swatch over the frame of an item. The frame will temporarily take on the colour of the swatch. Release the mouse button to apply the colour. Move the swatch away from an item if you do not wish to alter its colour.

⑤ Choose an option in the % (Shade) pop-up menu.

Or:

② choose Frame… in the Item menu. The Frame Specifications dialog box will be displayed. Choose options in the Colour and Shade pop-up menus.

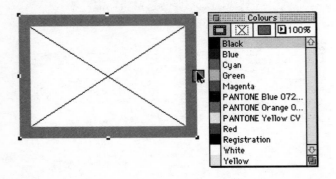

Colouring and shading box backgrounds

You can use the same drag-and-drop technique mentioned on the opposite page to alter the background colour of boxes. Alternatively you can alter the background colour and shade of selected boxes within the Text or Picture Box Specifications dialog box.

① With either the Item tool or Content tool active, select a text or picture box.

Either:

② choose Show Colours in the View menu. The Colours palette will be displayed.

③ Click the right-hand Background icon at the top of the palette.

④ Either: click on a colour name.

Or: click-drag a colour swatch over the background of an item. The background will temporarily take on the colour of the swatch. Release the mouse button to apply the colour. Move the swatch away from an item if you do not wish to alter its colour.

⑤ Choose an option in the % (Shade) pop-up menu.

Or:

② choose Modify… in the Item menu. The Text or Picture Box Specifications dialog box will be displayed. Choose options in the Background Colour and Shade pop-up menus.

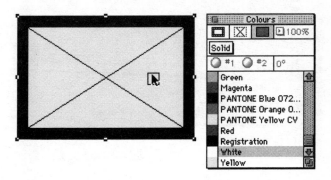

Colouring and shading lines

You can use the same drag-and-drop technique mentioned on the previous pages to alter the colour of lines. Alternatively you can alter the colour and shade of selected lines within the Style menu.

① With either the Item tool or Content tool active, select a line.

Either:

② choose Show Colours in the View menu. The Colours palette will be displayed.

③ The Line icon at the top of the palette will automatically be selected.

④ Either: click on colour name.

Or: click-drag a colour swatch over a line. The line will temporarily take on the colour of the swatch. Release the mouse button to apply a colour. Move the swatch away from a line if you do not wish to alter its colour.

⑤ Select an option in the % (Shade) pop-up menu.

Or:

② choose options in the Colour and Shade sub-menus in the Style menu.

Blending box backgrounds

Colours can be blended in text and picture box backgrounds to meet a variety of design needs.

① With the Item tool active, select a text or empty picture box.

② Choose Show Colours in the View menu. The Colours palette will be displayed.

③ Click the right-hand Background icon at the top of the palette.

④ Choose an option in the Blend pop-up menu.

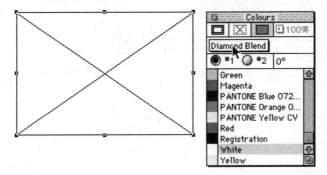

⑤ Click the #1 radio button. Click a colour name (not its swatch). This colour will be applied to the background.

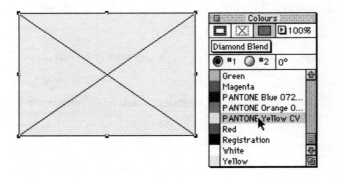

⑤ Click the #2 radio button. Click another colour name (not its swatch). This second colour will blend with the first colour to create a graduated effect. If you have the Content tool selected, deselect the box to activate blend or select the Item tool.

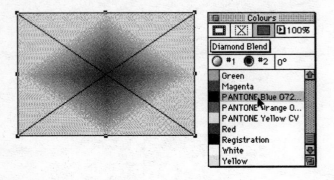

Colouring and shading pictures

① With the Content tool active, select an image in a picture box.

Either:

② choose Show Colours in the View menu. The Colours palette will be displayed.

③ Click the centre Image icon at the top of the palette.

④ Click on colour name.

⑤ Choose an option in the % (Shade) pop-up menu.

Or:

② choose options in the Colour and Shade sub-menus in the Style menu.

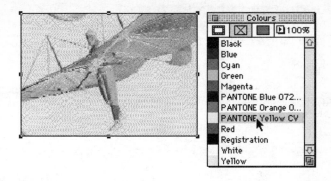

Some picture types which you can colour

	Image		Background	
Type	*colour*	*shade*	*colour*	*shade*
Bitmapped images:				
Line (1-bit) PICT/TIFF	●	●	●	●
Grayscale (8-bit) PICT/TIFF	●	○	●	○
Colour (24-bit) PICT/TIFF	○	○	○	○
Vector images:				
PICT, EPS	○	○	○	○

Colouring and shading text

①   With the Content tool active, select the text to be coloured.

     Either:

②   choose Show Colours in the View menu. The Colours palette will be displayed.

③   Click the centre Text icon at the top of the palette.

④   Click on a colour name and select an option in the % (Shade) pop-up menu.

     Or:

②   choose options in the Colour and Shade sub-menus in the Style menu.

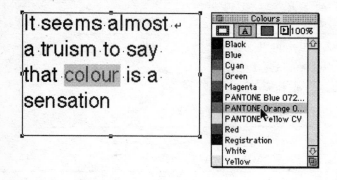

Managing colours

Basing colours on existing colours

① Choose Colours… in the Edit menu. The Colours for … dialog box will be displayed.

② Select a colour in the Colours list. Click Duplicate.

③ Alter the CMYK mixes or choose another Pantone colour in the same way as you create a colour from scratch.

The New and Old boxes will display the colours for comparison purposes.

④ Type in a new name in the Name field (for CMYK model only). The Pantone name will be amended automatically when you choose a new colour.

③ Click OK. Click Save.

▲ Use this approach when you wish to create a colour that will work well with an existing colour.

Amending colours

① Choose Colours… in the Edit menu. The Colours for … dialog box will be displayed.

② Select a colour in the Colours list. Click Edit.

③ Alter the CMYK mixes or choose another Pantone colour in the same way as you create a colour from scratch.

The New and Old boxes will display any colour change for comparison purposes.

③ Click OK. Click Save.

Copying colours from other documents

① Choose Colours… in the Edit menu. The Colours for … dialog box will be displayed.

② Click Append. The Append Colours directory dialog box will be displayed.

③ Locate the document (with the colours) in the Append Colours directory dialog box.

④ Click Open. The colours will be added to the Colours list.

⑤ Click Save.

———— Registering colours ————

Hairline gaps can sometimes appear between coloured items when documents are printed on web offset printing presses. This is due to colour mis-registration.

QuarkXPress automatically compensates for such mis-registration by slightly overlapping abutted colours.

Trapping, the term used to describe this process, is applied by QuarkXPress only when files are colour-separated for output to film. No trapping takes place when documents are printed on composite grayscale and colour printers so there's no need to worry about trapping settings when outputting on these devices.

You can enter trapping settings yourself in the Trapping Preferences dialog box or you can let the bureau handle this for you. Any settings must be agreed by your printer who alone knows the optimum trapping amounts for individual documents.

Preparing items for trapping

Automatic trapping only takes place if items are considered by QuarkXPress to be overlapping. If you do not intend items to touch, ensure there is a small gap between them, otherwise trapping may appear to butt the items together.

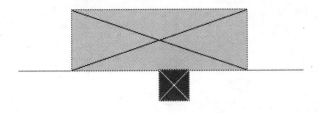

Overlapping coloured items

Either:

● position coloured items so they are very slightly overlapping.

Or:

● snap coloured items to a common ruler guide.

Summary

● **Always refer to colour reference books when creating new colours.**

● **Use either the CMYK or one of the Pantone models to create colours.**

● **Uncheck Process Separations if you wish a colour to be printed as a spot colour.**

● **Use the Colours palette to apply colours quickly to items, text and images.**

● **Discuss trapping with your bureau if you are planning to imageset a coloured document.**

12

IMPROVING THE
APPEARANCE
OF YOUR WORK

This chapter covers:

- the H&Js dialog box
- the Find/Change dialog box
- the Font Usage dialog box
- the Formats dialog box

——— Hyphenating words ———

Both justified text with overwide word spacing and unjustified text with very ragged line lengths can look unsightly. Such 'horrors' can be reduced through the judicious use of hyphenation. Hyphenation can be inserted automatically or you can do it manually.

Automatic hyphenation is controlled by the Standard H&J by default, is global and does not differentiate between different alignments. For this reason you should turn it off.

Once this has been done, you can hyphenate words yourself using special discretionary hyphens.

Disabling auto hyphenation

①   Choose H&Js... in the Edit menu. The H&Js for... dialog box will be displayed.

②   Select Standard in the H&Js list and click Edit. The Edit Hyphenation & Justification dialog box will be displayed.

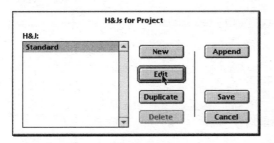

③   Uncheck the Auto Hyphenation box.

④   Click OK. Click Save.

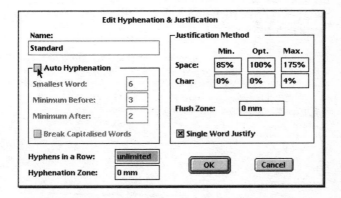

▲   If you wish to apply automatic hyphenation selectively within a document, create a new H&J and check Auto Hyphenation. Apply the new H&J by choosing it in the H&Js pop-up menu in the Paragraphs Formats dialog box when formatting paragraphs.

Hyphenating locally

Break the first word in each line immediately following an over-spaced or short line using special discretionary hyphens. Unlike ordinary hyphens, these hyphens automatically disappear if a word no longer needs to be broken as a result of subsequent editing work.

Inserting discretionary hyphens

① Position the insertion point within the first word of a line.

② Press ⌘+-. The word will hyphenate if sufficient space is available in the above line to accommodate the part word.

③ If nothing happens, position the insertion point further left in the word and try step two again.

Gaining advice on where to hyphenate

① Position the insertion point within the word.

② Choose Suggested Hyphenation… in the Utilities menu. The Suggested Hyphenation box will be displayed with possible hyphen positions.

▲ Try to avoid hyphenating words within unjustified alignments as hyphens can often is look worse than the ragged lines they replace. Short captions, and text areas composed of mainly short lines and, maybe many names (such as catalogue entries) should always be unhyphenated and unjustified (either with left, centred or right alignments).

— Removing widows and orphans —

Removing widows in paragraphs

Widows are short lines (strictly 6 characters or less) at ends of paragraphs. Because of their short length they sometimes can make text look a bit untidy. Their removal not only neatens text but also reduces the numbers of lines in a text box, which may or may not be beneficial.

Paragraph with widow   Paragraph with widow removed

Removing widows without editing text

①   With the Content tool active, select the whole paragraph.

②   Choose Track… in the Style menu and enter a figure of up to -5. If the tracking is currently a positive figure, say 8, apply a tracking figure of up to 5 units less, such as 3.

③   Click OK.

Avoiding orphans at column extremities

Orphans are last lines of paragraphs positioned by chance at top and bottoms of text boxes.

If they are short in length they can upset the visual alignment of columns, making it appear that the columns are not horizontally aligned.

Like widows, they can also look untidy so it's best where possible to prevent them from appearing.

Orphans are eliminated by keeping the the first and last two lines of paragraphs together. So instead of a word appearing at, say, the top of a linked box or column, the line preceding the potential orphan also moves up to the top, thereby providing a first full line of text.

This leaves an empty last line in the previous column which can be filled, if so desired, by adding an additional line in the column by whatever means appropriate.

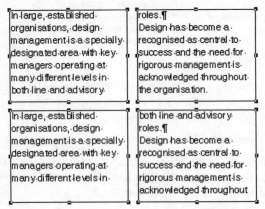

Top: last line of paragraph creates an unsatisfactory first line.
Above: preceding line moves up to create a better first line.

Avoiding orphans automatically

① With the Content tool active, select a paragraph or paragraphs.

② Choose Formats… in the Style menu. The Paragraph Formats dialog box will be displayed.

③ Check Keep Lines Together. Click Start and enter 2 in the Start and End fields.

④ Click OK.

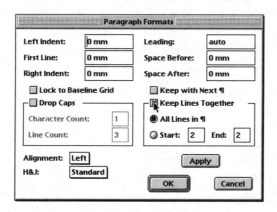

Removing 'rivers' in paragraphs

Rivers are unsightly gaps running more or less vertically in areas of text caused by the incidence of large adjacent words spaces.

Remove 'rivers' by negative tracking – see *Removing widows in paragraphs* (page 143) or by applying local hyphenation – see *Hyphenating locally* (page 142).

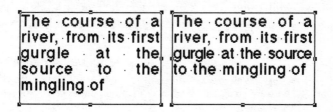

Improving readability

Improving leading

Almost all text is made more readable by the addition of leading. It alters the colour (texture) of text areas and makes the text more accessible.

If you feel paragraphs can be improved through the adjustment of leading, alter the leading locally within paragraphs or, if you have used style sheets in your document, amend the leading within individual style sheets.

Use minimal leading values for very short lines of text, equal to or slightly *greater* than the font size.

Also use minimal leading values for large headings, equal to or slightly *less* than the font size.

Lines of eight to ten words in length normally require leading which roughly corresponds to 110% of the font size. Longer lines, of course, require proportionately more leading.

Setting readable line lengths

The optimum number of characters per line of continuous text varies considerably between types of documents. In books, 60–70 would represent a good basis to work from. You can try a larger number of characters per line than this, with generous leading, and it may work; certainly anything above 90 characters per line will be too much.

In news articles, between 30 and 45 characters per line is the norm.

Text with a low character count tends to look racy, readable and accessible, whilst text with a high character count tends to look more formal and perhaps more imposing, although much depends on other factors.

If you wish to alter the character count in paragraphs, either alter the width of text areas and/or alter the size of fonts. Alter the font size locally within paragraphs or, if you have used style sheets in your document, amend the font size within individual style sheets.

– Adjusting word and letter spacing –

Maintaining good word and character spacing

Use standard tracking (zero units of track) for normal text areas. Occasionally, some slight closing-up (negative tracking) or slight widening (positive tracking) may be appropriate in text. Ideally tracking should not be vary within a paragraph.

Text in very small font sizes, around 6 or 7 pt, can be slightly widened on occasions to improve legibility.

In display sizes, of say 18 pt and above, some slight closing-up (negative tracking) is often desirable, otherwise the work looks too 'gappy'.

Improving spacing in justified alignments

Word and character spacing within justified paragraphs is controlled by the Standard H&J by default and is global. The justification settings have a marked effect on the look of text and should be set to allow for a reasonable amount of variation in word spacing, with limited variation in inter-character spacing.

① Choose H&Js... in the Edit menu. The H&Js for... dialog box will be displayed.

② Select Standard in the H&Js list and click Edit. The Edit Hyphenation & Justification dialog box will be displayed.

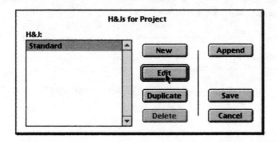

④ Alter the values in the Justification method fields to match the illustration.

④   Click OK. Click Save.

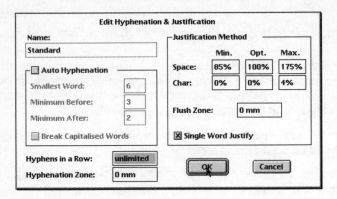

Improving the spacing between characters

You can correct poor spacing between individual characters within large headings by kerning. Like tracking, kerning is measured as percentages of an en space. Unkerned inter-character spaces are set at 0.

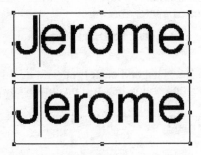

Top: the characters J and e are too close.
Above: the letters are kerned to increase
the spacing between them.

Adjusting inter-character spaces

①   Position the insertion point between two characters within a word. The text should not be highlighted in any way.

②   Choose Kern… in the Style menu and enter a figure in the Kern dialog box.
A positive figure, such as 5 will widen the inter-character spacing; a negative figure such as –5 will tighten the inter-character spacing.

▲   Only kern badly-spaced characters in very large font sizes, say over 36 pt. It's usually unnecessary to kern smaller sizes as any poor inter-character spacing is less disturbing to the eye.

———— Cleaning up text ————

Eliminating typing errors

If you wish to remove all instances of double spaces, spaces before full points and other errors, use the Find/Change function within the Edit menu.

①   Select the Content tool but do not select a text box.

②   Choose Find/Change… in the Edit menu.

③   Type in the character(s) to be found in the Find what field and replacement character(s), if any, in the Change to field.

④   Check the Document box to find and change all text within the document.

⑤   Click Find Next to find the first instance of the character(s) and click Replace if you wish to replace the character(s).

⑥   Click Find Next again and repeat the process until all instances of the characters have been replaced.

⑦   Close the dialog box.

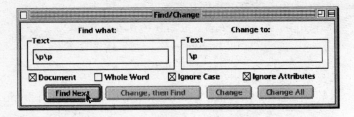

Entering invisibles in the Find/Change dialog box

Type the codes or use the following keystrokes to enter invisibles into the Text fields.

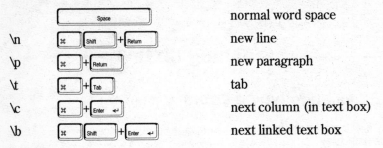

	Space	normal word space
\n	⌘ Shift + Return	new line
\p	⌘ + Return	new paragraph
\t	⌘ + Tab	tab
\c	⌘ + Enter ↵	next column (in text box)
\b	⌘ Shift + Enter ↵	next linked text box

Eliminating wrong fonts

You can easily identify and replace incorrectly-used fonts before outputting your document.

① Choose a scale in the View menu which enables you to read all your document text easily.

② Choose Font Usage... in the Utilities menu.The Font Usage dialog box will be displayed.

③ View the fonts you've used in the Find what pop-up menu. If all your fonts are present and correct, close the dialog box. If a font is listed which you did not intend to use, follow the next steps.

④ Choose any wrong font in the Find what pop-up menu.

⑤ Choose a suitable replacement font in the Change to pop-up menu.

⑥ Click Find Next. The first instance of the wrong font will be shown.

⑦ Click Change if you wish to change the font. If the currently chosen replacement font is unsuitable, choose another font in the Change to pop-up menu beforehand.

⑧ Repeat steps 3 and 4 until all the wrong fonts have been replaced.

⑨ Close the Font Usage dialog box.

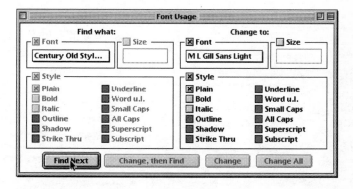

▲ The Font Usage dialog box is one reference point for listing fonts for your bureau (if you do not use Collect for Output).

Summary

- Maintain an even texture in all text areas.

- Apply hyphenation locally within most documents.

- Avoid hyphenating text which is left, centred or right aligned.

- Remove widows and orphans and unsightly word spacing as a matter of course.

- Kern large text if the inter-character spacing is irregular.

- Use generous leading for paragraphs with long lines set in small font sizes.

13

PREPARING FILES
FOR PRINTING

This chapter covers:

- the Picture Usage dialog box
- the Font Usage dialog box
- the Chooser
- the Print dialog box
- the Page Setup dialog box
- the Picture Box Specifications dialog box
- the Collect for Output directory dialog box

QuarkXPress documents can be printed using desktop printers or large digital colour printers (such as Canon printers). They can also be imageset at a bureau to produce bromide or film for subsequent photo litho printing.

Whichever method of output you employ, picture links need to be checked prior to final output and if you are outputting from a computer other than your own, you will also need to check the font usage.

– Outputting from another computer –

Checking picture links

When you include images in a QuarkXPress document, links are automatically established between individual images within your document and their originals.

When you output your document, QuarkXPress uses the data in the original files to reproduce the images, unless the images have been saved in PICT format, in which case it uses the embedded file. If it's unable to locate and use the original files, QuarkXPress will use the data in the embedded images for reproduction purposes. Reproduction by this means is inferior but may be adequate for printing or for proofing purposes.

If links between the images and their original files are inadvertently broken, they can easily be re-established using the Picture Usage dialog box. It's important, in any case, to check the status of all links on completion of a document, whether or not you think any links are broken.

Checking picture linkage

① Choose Picture Usage… in the Utilities menu. The Picture Usage dialog box will be displayed.

② Look at the status column for each picture. The status will be OK, Modified or Missing.

If the status in all cases is OK, there is no need for you to do anything so close the dialog box.

If the status of any picture is Missing, select the file name and click Update. The Find "…" directory dialog box will be displayed. Locate and select the missing picture file using the directory dialog box controls. Click Open.

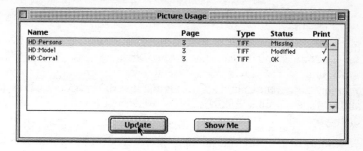

If the status of any picture is Modified, select the file name and click Update. An alert dialog box saying 'OK to update "..."?' will be displayed.

③ Close the dialog box.

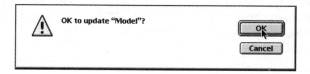

✦ OK status means the document is properly linked to an unmodified picture file.

Modified status means the document is properly linked to a modified picture file.

Missing status means the document is not linked anymore to the picture file originally imported. This is usually because the file has since been moved or renamed.

Checking font usage

When your document is output, QuarkXPress uses the fonts loaded on the outputting computer. If your document uses non-system fonts, QuarkXPress will ask for suitable substitute fonts if the specified fonts are not available. This almost invariably occurs when documents are output at a bureau.

If you restrict your font usage to the Macintosh system fonts, you should have no problem in this regard. The system fonts include Chicago, Courier, Geneva, Helvetica, Monaco, New York, Times and Zapf Dingbats. Obviously you won't be able to restrict yourself to these fonts for most jobs. So if you are planning to imageset your document and you wish to use fonts other than System fonts, use only Adobe Type 1 fonts.

Where possible, avoid Truetype fonts as they perform less reliably on PostScript devices. Purely bitmap (non-outline) fonts should also be avoided unless the font size corresponds to one of the sizes shown as outline in the Size menu.

Checking font usage

①   Choose Font Usage... in the Utilities menu. The Font Usage dialog box will be displayed.

②   View the fonts you've used in the Find what pop-up menu.

③   Close the dialog box.

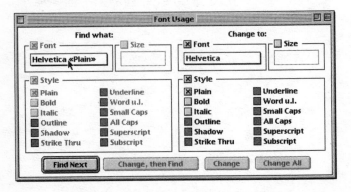

▲   The Font Usage dialog box is a useful reference point when listing fonts for your bureau (if you do not use Collect for Output).

Printing documents

Logging into a printer

① Choose Chooser in the Apple menu.

② Click the driver of the printer you wish to use, in the top left window.

③ Select a zone (if your printer is networked) in the bottom left window.

④ Click the printer listed in the right window.

⑤ Click the Close box.

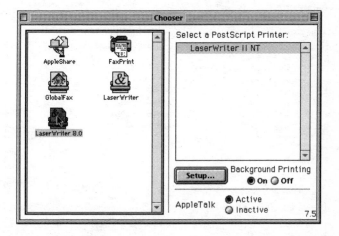

❗ Ensure that AppleTalk is active in the Chooser, otherwise your computer will not be able to communicate with the printer.

Specifying the page setup

When you print, you need first to inform your printing device about the document's page setup.

① Choose Page Setup... in the File menu. The Page Setup dialog box will be displayed.

② Choose the paper size you wish to use for printing by clicking a radio button option or choosing an option in the Paper pop-up menu.

③ Enter a value in the Reduce or Enlarge... % field. This option may not be available on a non-PostScript printer.

④ Click an Orientation option to suit your document.

⑤ Close the dialog box.

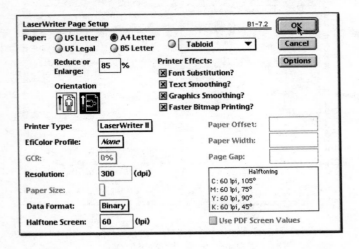

Previewing a document

●   Choose Hide Guides and Hide Invisibles in the View menu. If an item is already hidden the word Show will replace the word Hide so there is no need to choose the command.

Printing a document

①   Choose Print… in the File menu. The Print dialog box will be displayed. Note that the contents of this dialog box may differ from our illustration.

②   Enter the number of copies of each page required in the Copies field.

③   Under Pages, click the All radio button or enter a sequence of pages in the From and To fields.

④   Uncheck Collate if you wish multiple copies of pages to be printed together. This is the more efficient, faster way to print but will mean you will have to collate your documents by hand. Check Collate if you wish sets of documents to be printed together. This is the less efficient, slower way to print.

⑤   Choose either Centred or Off Centre in the Registration pop-up menu if you wish trim marks to print. Otherwise select Off.

⑥   Check Print Colours as Greys if you are printing a coloured document on a black and white (grayscale) printer. Otherwise leave unchecked.

⑦   Uncheck Spreads for printing pages on separate sheets of paper. Check Spreads for printing adjacent pages together on the same sheet of paper. If you select the latter option, ensure the paper size and scale in Page Setup is set to accommodate two pages side by side.

⑧   All other settings should correspond to those in the illustrated dialog box.

⑨   Click Print.

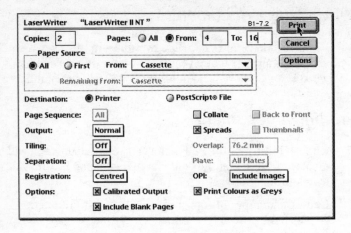

Printing large document pages in sections

If you are printing document pages larger than the paper in your printer, and you wish to print the pages full size, it's possible to print each page in sections. Once the sections are printed, you can tape them together to recreate each page.

① Position the Ruler Origin at the top left corner of the image area to be printed. See *Moving the ruler zero points* (page 31).

② Choose Print... in the File menu. The Print dialog box will be displayed. Note that the contents of this dialog box may differ from our illustration.

③ Choose Manual in the Tiling pop-up menu. The current position of the ruler origin will determine the top left corner of the image area to be printed.

④ Click Print.

⑤ Reposition the ruler origin so that it is at the top left corner of the next area of the document page you wish to print.

⑥ Choose Print... again in the File menu. The Print dialog box will be displayed.

⑦ Click Print.

⑧ Repeat steps 5–7 to seven until all the areas of the page have been printed.

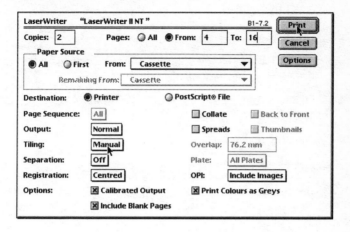

Shortening proofing times

If your document includes a large number of images, printing times will inevitably be long. You can shorten printing times by excluding images in a number of ways.

Omitting selected images and picture boxes

① Select individual picture boxes with either the Content tool or Item tool active.

② Choose Modify… in the Item menu. The Picture Box Specifications dialog box will be displayed.

③ Either: check the Suppress Picture Printout box to omit image only.

Or: check the Suppress Printout box to omit both image and picture box.

④ Click OK.

Omitting selected images

① Choose Picture Usage... in the Utilities menu. The Picture Usage dialog box will be displayed.

② Click to untick pictures in the Print column if you don't wish them to print.

③ Close the dialog box.

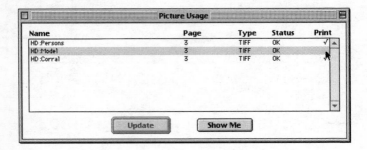

Omitting all TIFFs and/or EPS when printing

① Choose Print... in the File menu. The dialog box for your printer will be displayed. Note that the contents of this dialog box may differ from our illustration.

② Choose either Omit TIFF or Omit TIFF and EPS in the OPI pop-up menu.

③ Click Print.

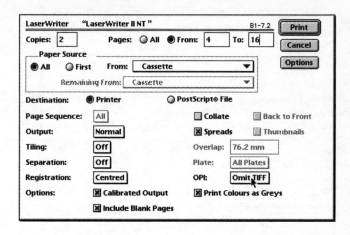

Omitting or printing all images at low resolution

① Choose Print... in the File menu. The dialog box for your printer will be displayed. Note that the contents of this dialog box may differ from our illustration.

② Either: choose Rough in the Output pop-up menu to omit images within picture boxes.

Or: choose Low Resolution in the Output pop-up menu to print images at 72 dpi (ppi).

③ Click Print.

───────── Working with OPI ─────────

Open Press Interface (OPI) enables the automatic substitution of low-resolution TIFF and EPS images for high-resolution versions when outputting within 'high-end' pre-press systems.

One of the key benefits of OPI is that it removes the need for you to hold large files on your computer drives.

When images are scanned for OPI, two versions of each image are made, one low-resolution and one high-resolution. The low-resolution images are created for layout purposes; the high-resolution images for outputting purposes. OPI comments are included in both files.

When either Omit TIFF or Omit TIFF and EPS is selected in the OPI pop-up menu in the Print dialog box, only the positional, scaling and cropping information of images is sent to the imagesetter.

The OPI interpreter reads the OPI comments in the low-resolution files and makes the substitution.

Omitting the redundant low-resolution picture data speeds processing times and reduces costs.

If OPI is used, it's best to convert those images which are not intended to be substituted for different file formats. For example if only TIFFs are to be substituted, ensure all other files are EPS.

OPI is only suitable for documents containing a large number of images with schedules which allow for all the scanning to take place prior to page layout work.

Using OPI

①   For every image in your document, specify:

      The document width and height in mm (as in Document setup), or percentage reduction/ enlargement.

      Whether it is to be reproduced in line, grayscale or colour.

②   Send all prints and transparencies to your bureau for scanning and OPI work. Note that not all bureaux employ OPI technology.

③   Import the low-resolution images you receive from the bureau/printer into your document using the normal Get Picture method.

④   Complete your document production work and submit your document and associated files to your bureau in the usual way.

——— Copying files for output ———

If you are proofing, printing or imagesetting your document at a bureau, the bureau will need a final copy of your document and all associated files, unless they have been saved in PICT format.

There are two ways to copy files. One way is to copy them manually to disk. Another way is to use Collect for Output, QuarkXPress's way of automatically copying files to disk.

The manual way has one major advantage: you can copy across files in their folders so all your files remain in an organised structure.

In theory, Collect for Output guarantees that all files are copied irrespective of their location on your computer. In the copying and collection process, all the files are brought together into a single folder. Because of this, try to make sure all your images have unique names, otherwise they may be renamed during the collection process.

Collect for Output produces a report in a text file format covering essential document information, Xtensions, fonts, graphic, style sheets, H&Js, colours, trapping, colour plates and so on. This checklist can be printed out by yourself and your bureau/printer.

Collecting pictures for output

① Choose Collect for Output... in the File menu. The Collect for Output directory dialog box will be displayed.

② Name the Report in the name field.

③ Select or create a folder (directory) on the disk in which to copy the QuarkXPress document and all its associated files.

④ Click Collect.

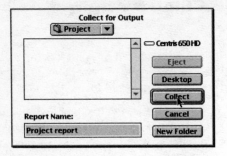

Copying files to disk using the Finder

①　Either: insert a double-sided, high density floppy into your disk drive.

Or: mount a Syquest or other large ejectable disk onto your Desktop.

②　Click-drag the folders containing your QuarkXPress document and associated files on your hard drive onto the icon of the floppy or ejectable disk. The files will be copied onto the disk.

③　Click-drag the floppy or ejectable disk icon into the Wastebasket. The floppy or ejectable disk will be ejected/unmounted.

—— What a bureau needs to know ——

Outputting to bromide

Inform the bureau about the following.

- Document Setup details:

  The document page size (in mm)

  Whether portrait or landscape orientation

- Page Setup details:

  Whether 100% scale or % reduction/enlargement

  The half-tone screen in lpi

- Print details:

  The pages to be output

  Whether registration marks are required

  Whether adjacent pages are to be printed as spreads

- Material details:

  That bromides are required

- Font details:

  Any non-system fonts used, including font type, founder's name, font name, variant and typestyle, such as PostScript, Monotype, Gill Bold, Italic

- Picture details:

  Picture types and number, such as EPS×5, TIFF×3

Outputting to colour prints

Inform the bureau about the following.

- Document Setup details:

   The document page size (in mm)

   Whether portrait or landscape orientation

- Page Setup details:

   Whether 100% scale or % reduction/enlargement

   The size of the paper to be printed on (A4 or larger)

- Print details:

   The pages to be output

   Whether registration marks are required

   Whether adjacent pages are to be printed as spreads

- Material details:

   That digital colour prints are required

- Font details:

   Any non-system fonts used, including font type, founder's name, font name, variant and typestyle, such as PostScript, Monotype, Gill Bold, Italic

- Picture details:

   Picture types and number, such as EPS×5, TIFF×3

Outputting to colour separations

Inform the bureau about the following.

- Document Setup details:

  The document page size (in mm)

  Whether portrait or landscape orientation

- Page Setup details:

  Whether 100% scale or % reduction/enlargement

  The half-tone screen in lpi

- Print details:

  The pages to be output

  That registration marks will be required

  Whether adjacent pages are to be printed as spreads or imposed for printing plates. If the latter is proposed, the imposition to be supplied by printer.

- Material details:

  That film positive or negatives are required, emulsion side down or up.

- Font details:

  Any non-system fonts used, including font type, founder's name, font name, variant and typestyle, such as PostScript, Monotype, Gill Bold, Italic

- Picture details:

  Picture types and number, such as EPS×5, TIFF×3

- Colour details:

  The printing plates used, such as cyan, magenta, yellow, black and Pantone Reflex Blue.

Summary

- Always check picture and font usage when completing a document.

- Shorten proofing times by omitting images.

- Use Collect for Output for copying files to disk.

- Give your bureau all the information they need to imageset a job accurately.

APPENDIX I

———————— Measurements ————————

Font sizes

Fonts are sized in points (a unit measuring 0.353 mm). A font size refers to the height of the body of a font and not the printed height (the body height can be seen when text is selected). Thus a 10 pt font has a body height of 10 pt and an overall printed height of fractionally less.

Leading

Leading is also measured in points. Leading refers to the distance from the baseline of one line of type to the next within a paragraph (the baseline is the imaginary line running along the bottom of those letters without descenders, such as an x).

The word 'leading' derives from the slivers of lead used to space out lines of metal type. Leading is expressed as the sum of the font size and leading thickness.

When the leading size is the same as the font size, the font is said to be unleaded. When the leading size is smaller, negative leading takes place (this would have been impossible with metal type).

Auto leading is pre-set at 120% of the font size and should only be used when initially sizing fonts or for single lines in text boxes.

Horizontal measures

Margin and gutter measures are normally specified in millimetres and paragraph indents in points. Paragraph indents are usually based on multiples or divisions of the font size, such as an em.

Vertical measures

Spaces before and after paragraphs and the offset of paragraph rules are normally measured in millimetres, points or alternatively, in the case of rules, expressed as a percentage of paragraph spaces. Spaces are usually based on multiples or divisions of the leading.

Word spaces

Normal word spaces, created using the space bar only, are approximately 0.5 en wide depending on the font and are subject to enlargement and reduction in justified setting. If you wish to maintain their width in selected situations, such as beside bullet points, use a word fixed space (see *Special characters* (page 169)).

✦ An en is equal to half the font size and corresponds roughly to the width of a lower-case n, from which it derives its name. Thus a 10 pt en is 5 pt wide.

Wider spaces can be inserted using the keyboard. Inserting two en spaces beside each other creates the wider em space.

✦ An em is equal to the font size and corresponds roughly to the width of a capital M, from which it derives its name. Thus a 10 pt em is 10 pt wide.

Both en and fixed word spaces maintain their width in justified setting but are affected by kerning and tracking changes.

APPENDIX II

———— Special characters ————

Included in this appendix are the most common special characters. There are many more. If there's a character you wish to use and it's not listed, refer to Key Caps in the Apple menu.

If this does not help you, you may need to buy a special font.

Most of the characters are achieved by using the modifier keys together with other keys. These keys, ⌘, Alt, Shift and Control should be held down separately or in various combinations whilst another key is pressed.

Certain key combinations may not work, especially the ones which create accented characters This could mean you are using a keyboard setting other than the British one. Check the current keyboard setting in the Keyboard Control Panel. This panel is accessed via the Apple menu.

Quotation marks

"   Alt + { [opening double quotes

"   Alt Shift + { [closing double quotes

'   Alt + }]   opening single quote

'   Alt Shift + }]   closing single quote

❗ It is only necessary to use the above four sets of commands if the Smart Quotes box is unchecked in the Application Preferences dialog box.

Inch and foot marks

" | `Control` `Shift` + `" '` | Imperial inch mark

' | `Control` + `" '` | Imperial foot mark

! It is only necessary to use the above two sets of commands if the Smart Quotes box is checked in the Application Preferences dialog box.

Selected punctuation, characters and symbols

...	`Alt` + `: ,`	ellipsis
•	`Alt` + `* 8`	small bullet point
■	`N` (Zapf Dingbats font)	solid box
□	`N` (Zapf Dingbats, outlined)	outlined box
●	`L` (Zapf Dingbats font)	solid bullet point
○	`L` (Zapf Dingbats, outlined)	outlined bullet point
×	`Alt` + `Y` (Symbol font)	multiplication sign
fi	`Alt` `Shift` + `% 5`	ligature of f and i
fl	`Alt` `Shift` + `^ 6`	ligature of f and l
©	`Alt` + `G`	copyright mark
™	`Alt` + `@ 2`	trade mark
®	`Alt` + `R`	registered mark
°	`Alt` `Shift` + `* 8`	degree symbol
†	`Alt` + `T`	dagger
¢	`Alt` + `$ 4`	cent
¥	`Alt` + `Y`	yen
¿	`Alt` `Shift` + `? /`	opening question mark
¡	`Alt` + `! 1`	opening exclamation mark
/	`Alt` `Shift` + `! 1`	shallow slash for fractions

Special characters for the Find/Change dialog box

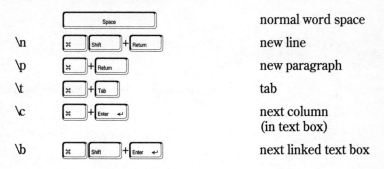

		normal word space
\n		new line
\p		new paragraph
\t		tab
\c		next column (in text box)
\b		next linked text box

Word spaces

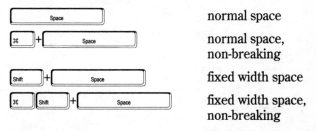

	normal space
	normal space, non-breaking
	fixed width space
	fixed width space, non-breaking

✚ A fixed width space is the same as a normal space but it maintains its width within justified alignments. See *Points of style* (page 177).

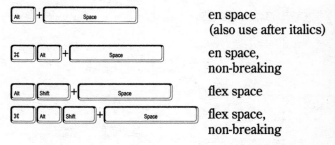

	en space (also use after italics)
	en space, non-breaking
	flex space
	flex space, non-breaking

✚ A flex space is a user-definable space. Enter 25% in the Flex Space Width field in the Typographic Preferences dialog box for a space approximately half the width of a standard word space. See *Points of style* (page 177).

Page numbers

⌘ + #3	page number code

Text commands

Return	paragraph return
Shift + Return	new line return
⌘ + Return	new line return, discretionary
⌘ + | \	indent following lines
Enter ↵	next column (in text box)
Shift + Enter ↵	next linked text box

Hyphens and dashes

-	–	hyphen
-	⌘ + –	hyphen, discretionary
–	Alt + –	en dash
—	Alt Shift + –	em dash

Accented letters

ç	Alt + C	cedilla
é	Alt + E, then E or other	acute
è	Alt + ~#, then E or other	grave
ü	Alt + U, then U or other	umlaut
ñ	Alt + N, then N or other	tilde
î	Alt + I, then I or other	circumflex

! For all the above six commands, press the Alt key with the letter and then press the appropriate character.

APPENDIX III

—————— Points of style ——————

Text areas with a clean, even texture (called colour), with thoughtful punctuation and simple formatting, not only look good but enhance readability and ensure good communication. So when detailing and formatting text, aim for simplicity and clarity at all times.

To help you achieve both of these qualities in your work, the following points of style have been suggested. They are intended as a guide; only refer to them in the absence of any other suitable house style.

Full points

Use the full point sparingly. Its main function is to denote the end of sentences. Only use them in other situations if their absence creates ambiguity.

Most abbreviations are unambiguous without full points.

Omit after contractions (Mr, Mrs, Dr, St, Ltd, and so on).

Omit after all common abbreviations: Esq, Rev, Co, Inc, mm, cm, km, kg, ms, ibid, per cent.

Omit after ft, yd, yds, cwt, oz, lb.

The word inch should be spelt out within sentences. In catalogues entries (especially if preceded or followed by metric equivalents) it can be abbreviated to 'in' without a full point.

Omit from mph, kph.

Omit from all groups of initials: BP, MIT, NEC, UK, UNICEF.

Omit from honours and awards: MA, PhD, FRIBA, MIEFE, DSO, CH.

Omit from post/zip codes.

Omit in BC, AD.

E*ither:* use p57, pp30–45s, vol18, fig625, p21, no5 with no full points but with half word space before figures (flex space set at 25%). *Or:* use p.63, pp.80–95, vol.89, fig.204, pl.4 3, no.6 with full point but no space after.

E*ither:* use *c*1900, *fh*1800, *d*1643 in italic with no full point and no space after. *Or:* use *c.*1900, *fl.*1800, *d.*1643 in italic with full point and no space after).

Format 6am, 11.30pm with half word space after figures (flex space set at 25%) and no full points either within or following am, pm.

Omit after initials before a surname and use normal word spacing: J C Bull, John C Bull. If you use full points, follow them by a half word space (flex space set at 25%): J.C.Bull, John C.Bull. Never close up initials.

Spell out Professor (not Prof.).

Omit from ranks: Lt Col, Maj Gen, Capt or, preferably, spell in full.

Omit from Rt Hon, MP.

Use an elipsis… *(not* full points...) as a tail off.

Commas

Omit after street numbers and between the name of city/town and the postal code.

Omit between a name and the honour/award, and between awards: C Hodder MA.

Dashes

Use en dashes '–' (not hyphens '-') with word spaces either side as a substitute for colons and parentheses.

Use em dashes '—' with or without word spaces either side as an alternative substitute for colons and parentheses, to indicate a pause between a full point and a comma or a change of thought.

Quotations

Either: use single quotation marks; double quotation marks for quotations within quotations. *Or:* use double quotation marks; single quotation marks for quotations within quotations.

Set long quotations in a smaller font size, without quotation marks, with a half line space before and after, with or without left and right indents. Alternatively, use the accompanying text size, with quotation marks, half line space before and after, and not indented. If the main text is justified, use left alignment without any indents.

Position full points and commas inside quotation marks. If the quotation is at the end of and part of a larger sentence, position the full point outside the quotation marks.

Position colons and semi-colons outside quotation marks.

Capitals, small capitals and non-aligning figures

Use non-aligning figures, if the font includes them in preference to aligning figures, except possibly within tables.

Use small capitals for groups of initials, postal codes (in combination with non-aligning figures), complete words or phrases in capitals within the text, and so on.

Avoid using capitals reduced in size within continuous text, as they will appear too light in relation to the lower-case letters.

Use small capitals for groups of initials consisting of more than three letters.

Countries should always be in full capitals: UK, USA.

If a group of initials is followed by a word commencing with a capital, this group is best in capitals: ICI Chemicals, not ICI Chemicals.

Format Roman numerals mostly in small capitals with capitals used only to give necessary weight.

Use capitals up to V, small capitals thereafter: vol IV, vols XVIII–XXII.

Use capitals for kings and queens: Elizabeth I, Henry VIII.

Format MS, MSS in small capitals with no full points.

Use small capitals, with lower case where necessary, for honours and awards: BSC, PhD.

Small capitals are usually set as a percentage of capitals but is alterable in the Typographic Preferences dialog box. The small capitals in this book are set at 85% of capitals size.

Numerals

Use from 500 to 600 or 500–600, *not* from 500–600. Use an en dash with a half word space (flex space set at 25%) space either side.

Dates: 1808-9 1808-12, 1820-21. Use a hyphen with a half word space (flex space set at 25%) on either side. Do not repeat the century: 1780-1820, 1720-30, but not 1820-1830.

Set 28 July 1946, in that order, no commas, no th or st, nd, rd.

Set 250 BC, but AD 250.

Set 18 ft, 21 mm with a half word space (flex space set at 25%).

Set 210×297 mm, $8 \times 2 \times 48$ in; 'mm' or 'in' to appear after final dimension, and should be preceded by a half word space (flex space set at 25%). The $\times$ should be set in Symbol (Alt-Y), be x-height, aligned on baseline and have half word spaces either side (flex spaces set at 25%). If the Symbol font is not available, use a lower case x, preferably from a sans serif font such as Helvetica.

Bullets and numbered lists

Use fixed width or en spaces between bullet/numbers and following text unless hanging indents are used.

APPENDIX IV

Key work stages

The way you work on documents will be influenced by a number of factors including the nature of the document in hand, the amount of work time you are allocated, the document's importance, personal preferences and such like.

There's no doubt that a structured step-by-step approach to document design and production not only enables you to be more efficient but also allows you to gain the maximum amount of pleasure from working with QuarkXPress.

For these two reasons, I include two typical processes, distilled from the many projects with which I have personally been involved.

The processes are not intended to be a straightjacket; just use them as a guide or checklist and a basis from which to develop processes more suited to your own needs.

Creating documents

Straightforward documents

① Set document size and grid in the New Document dialog box.

② Adjust document preferences, as required.

③ Insert additional document pages, as required.

④ Add ruler guides and items to Master A, common to *all* document pages.

⑤ Add ruler guides to document pages.

⑥ Produce page layouts with imported text and scanned images.

⑦ Check spelling, font and picture usage.

⑧ Print pages for evaluation and proofing.

Documents using resources from other documents

① Set document size and grid in the New Document dialog box.

② Adjust document preferences, as required.

③ Insert additional document pages, as required.

④ Add ruler guides and items common to all pages on Master A.

⑤ Add ruler guides to document pages.

⑥ Append colours, H&Js and Style Sheets from other documents in this order.

⑦ Create a library to place frequently-used items.

⑧ Produce page layouts with imported text and scanned images.

⑨ Check spelling, font and picture usage.

⑩ Print pages for evaluation and proof checking.

Creating templates

Stage one

① Set document size and grid in the New Document dialog box.

② Adjust document preferences, as required.

③ Insert additional document pages, as required.

④ Add ruler guides and items to Master A, common to *all* document pages.

⑤ Add ruler guides to document pages.

⑥ Create colours, adjust/create additional H&Js.

⑦ Create a library to place frequently-used items.

⑧ Add page items, text and images to individual pages, common to *all* issues.

⑨ Save the document as a Document in the usual way. Then Save As the document also as a Document under a different name.

Stage two

① Working on the second 'Saved As' document, produce *sample* page layouts with imported text and scanned images.

② Create Style Sheets from sample text.

③ Print the sample pages for evaluation and proof checking.

④ Save the document as a Document in the usual way. Close the document.

Stage three

① Open the original document.

② Append H&Js and Style Sheets from the second document in this order.

③ Save As the document as a Template under the same or a different name. Close the template.

④ Open the template to work on individual issues.

APPENDIX V

—————————— Glossary ——————————

Absolute page numbers numbers which refer to the sequence of pages in a document, starting from the first page

Adobe Type 1 fonts PostScript technology used by font manufacturers

Alert box dialog box on a screen alerting you to the consequences of a decision you are about to make

Backup in QuarkXPress, an automatically saved revision of a document

Baseline imaginary line on which upper and lower case letters sit; descenders extend below this line

Bitmapped image image made up of pixels (or dots)

Bromide photographic paper used by imagesetters for artwork quality prints

Body non-printing height of a font

Bit smallest possible unit of information; short for binary digit

Bureau company specialising in printing and/or imagesetting DTP documents. (In this book, bureau refers also to a repro department at a printing works and a colour copy shop.)

Character generic name for a letter, number, symbol or 'invisible'

Check box small box that works as a toggle for selecting an option. (When you click on an empty box, an X appears, turning it on; when you click again, the X disappears and the option is turned off.)

Chooser desk accessory used to log into devices, such as printers and other computers linked to a network; also used to enable and disable AppleTalk, Apple's native networking protocol

Clipboard area of a Macintosh's memory that holds what you last cut or copied; paste inserts a copy of the current contents of the Clipboard

CMYK stands for cyan, magenta, yellow and key (black), the colour model used in the graphic and printing fields

Column principal text and image areas, within the page margins

Copyfitting editing or formatting text to fit within prescribed text areas

Cursor a Latin word sometimes used to describe the pointer or the insertion point

Dialog box box on a screen requesting information, or a decision, from you

DTP short for Desktop Publishing

Drive floppy, removable or hard disk

Drop cap large capital letter integrated within the first few lines of a paragraph

En measure equal to half the width of the square of a font size e.g. a 15 pt en is 7.5 pt; used as a horizontal unit of measure – *see* em

Em measure equal to the width of the square of a font size e.g. a 15 pt en is 15 pt; used as a horizontal unit of measure – *see* en

Field in QuarkXPress, an area in a dialog box or palette in which you enter values

Film photographic film used by imagesetters for colour separations

Fixed space word space which doesn't vary in justified alignments

Flex space user-definable space which doesn't vary in justified alignments

Folder sub division (sub-directory) of a disk

Font typeface comprising a collection of letters, numbers, punctuation marks and symbols with an identifiable and consistent appearance

Fold crease dividing document pages, not to be confused with a bound spine

Founder company which commissions, designs, makes and markets fonts

Frame border around a text or picture box; a box rule

Grabber hand tool which allows you to move around a document without using the scroll bars

Grayscale depiction of grey tones between black and white; usually composed of 256 greys

Greek depiction of pictures and text as blocks of grey to speed screen redraw

Grid network of column, margin and ruler guides which define the major alignments and principal spaces on a page

Gutter vertical space between columns

Half-tone pattern (or screen) of dots of different sizes used to simulate a continuous tone photograph, either in colour or monochrome; measured in lines per inch

H&J short for Hyphenation and Justification: a function within QuarkXPress which controls the automatic hyphenation and justification of text within paragraphs

Hyphenation breaking of words into two parts to improve word spacing

I Beam pointer's shape when dealing with text

Image graphic, photograph or illustration

Imagesetter digital phototypesetting machine capable of producing graphic images as well as type on bromide or film (Most imagesetters are PostScript-compatible.)

Indent set back of lines of text in a paragraph, measured in QuarkXPress from the text box inset

Insertion point blinking vertical line indicating where the next keystroke will add or delete text

Invisibles characters which don't print, such as [Tab] and [Shift]

Item in QuarkXPress, text, picture box or line

Justification alignment of text at both sides of a paragraph through the adjustment of word spacing

Kerning in QuarkXPress, inter-character spacing adjusted locally at a character level; used for styling, and optical reasons

Keystrokes use of modifier keys with other keys to execute a command

Keypad numeric keys on the right of the keyboard

Leading distance between lines of text, usually measured between baselines

Line printed rule; images which contain black and white areas, without intervening greys

lpi short for lines per inch; the measurement of a half-tone screen

Margin outer area of the page surrounding the principal text and image areas

Master page pages which provide document pages with their column and margin guides

Master page items items on document pages provided by master pages

Menu list of commands

Modifier keys keys which modify the effect of a character key: standard modifier keys are ⌘, Alt, Shift, Control and Caps Lock.

OPI short for Open Press Interface

Orthogonal line which is either horizontal or vertical

Page one side of a leaf in a document

Palette small movable box containing commands

Pantone Matching System PMS for short; proprietory colour matching system used in the graphics and printing industries

Paragraph in QuarkXPress, any text separated by Return

Pasteboard temporary storage and work area outside the page, the contents of which don't print out

Photo litho short for photo lithography; the primary printing technology used in the printing industry

PICT Apple's native file format

Point unit of measure; approximately 0.353 mm

Process colours the CMYK colours used to reproduce colour photographs and illustrations

Program group of instructions that tells a computer what to do; also called software

Printer digital desktop or commercial device for printing or proofing documents primarily using laser, ink jet, die sublimation and thermal wax technologies

PostScript Adobe's page description language used by QuarkXPress and other DTP programs

QuickDraw programming routines that enable the Macintosh to display graphic elements on screen; also used to output text and images to certain non-PostScript printers – *see* PostScript

Radio buttons group of small buttons for selecting an option, one of which can be on at any one time

Registration marks marks included on film separations for purposes of colour registration

Remapping rearranging the dots within a bitmapped image

Resolution in this book, the amount of data in a scanned image, measured in pixels (or dots) per linear inch

RGB stands for red, green, blue; the colour model used by monitors and within multimedia documents

Rivers unsightly gaps running vertically within text

Runaround in QuarkXPress, the feature which controls the way text is displaced by boxes and images

Running head header

Scan bitmapped image created by scanner

Scroll bars bars equipped with a scroll box and scroll arrows which enable you to scroll vertically or horizontally within windows

Special colour *see* Spot colour

Spine binding edge of a document; part of a document's cover which is visible when placed on a shelf

Spot colour colours other than the process colours printed as a separate colour within a photo litho printed document; sometimes called Special colour

Style sheets stored grouping of text formats used to format paragraphs quickly and accurately

System fonts fonts which come standard with Macintosh computers

Template document with special content which you use repeatedly; you can modify and/or add to it and save it under a different name

TIFF short for Tagged Image File Format, the defacto file format for saving scanned images

Tiling printing document pages in sections

Tracking in QuarkXPress, word and letter spacing adjusted locally at a character level; used for copyfitting, styling and to improve readability

Trapping technique use to minimise the effects of the mis-registration of photo litho printing on a printed document

Trim marks lines printed outside the edge of a document page for aligning guillotines

Truetype fonts Apple's own font technology used by the system fonts

Typography craft of designing with type

Window enclosed area on the screen in which a document appears

WP short for word processing

Vectored drawing or object defined mathematically; sometimes called object orientated

XTension third party program which extends the functionality of QuarkXPress

Keys

`Alt` Alt key – a modifier key used in conjection with other keys, often providing an alternative function; by itself it activates the Grabber Hand

`Delete` Back space/Delete key – used to delete text to the left of the insertion point, selected text and items

`⌘` Command key (with an Apple on it) – a modifier key used with other keys to issue commands. By itself it activates the Item tool, when the Content tool is active

`Control` Control key – a modifier key used in conjection with other keys. By itself it activates the Zoom tool

`⌦` Delete key – used to delete text to the right of the insertion point

`Enter ↵` Enter key – used to move text, close dialog boxes and implement field values in the Measurements palette, amongst other things

`Return` Return key – used to separate paragraphs, close dialog boxes and implement field values in the Measurements palette

`Shift` Shift key – a modifier key used to capitalise letters and constrain pointer movement, amongst other things

`Tab` Tab key – keystroke which moves the insertion point to the next tab position, by default 0.5 in apart.

Index

Apple, 41, 118, 157, 173, 185, 188–189

box shapes
creating polygons, 97–98
border
frames, 80, 105, 110, 129–130
box rule
frames, 80, 105, 110, 129–130
colours
adding, 125
cmyk model, 126–127, 137
Pantone model, 126, 128
process, 3, 123–125, 127–128, 138–139, 188–189
spot (special), 125–126
colouring
blending, 133
box frames, 130
box backgrounds, 129, 131, 133
lines, 129, 132
managing, 137
paragraph rules, 129
pictures, 129, 134
picture types, 135
registering, 138
text, 136
trapping, 138–139, 165, 189
clipboard, 33, 36, 39–41, 45, 91, 95–96, 100–101, 105, 109, 186

characters
font, 62, 140, 151–153, 156, 167–169, 171–173, 179, 185–186, 189
size, 8, 47–48, 51, 62, 73, 146–147, 156, 171–172, 179, 186
typestyle, 61, 167–169
kern, 8, 149, 152
track, 8, 57, 143, 147
columns
master pages, 89
text boxes, 69–71

directory dialog boxes
Collect for Output, 151, 153, 156, 165, 170
Open, 16, 19, 120
Get Picture, 106
Get Text, 39
Save, 13, 15–16, 20
Save as, 15–16, 20
dialog boxes
Application Preferences., 10, 17–18, 38, 42, 105, 124, 173–174
Check Document, 45
Document Setup, 27
Edit Colours, 126–127
Find/Change, 42
Frame Specifications, 80, 111, 130
Font Usage, 151, 156

TEACH YOURSELF

PHOTOSHOP

Adobe Photoshop has become *the* tool for preparing and manipulating photographs and other still images for desktop publishing and multimedia documents. In *Teach Yourself Photoshop* Christopher Lumgair introduces you to the essentials of the program, guiding you through the scanning, image preparation and enhancement basics in easy-to-follow stages, concentrating on techniques which will enable you to create well-crafted images with the minimum of effort.

This book
- has clear, informative and jargon-free text
- assumes no previous knowledge of the program
- is written by a professional graphic designer and experienced trainer
- combines essential techniques with guidance on the best way to scan and manipulate still images.

Christopher Lumgair has a BA in Graphic Design and has spent several years working in magazine and book publishing. He now has his own successful digital publishing consultancy.